THE MARY
WHITEHOUSE
EXPERIENCE
ENCYCLOPEDIA

THE MARY
WHITEHOUSE
EXPERIENCE
ENCYCLOPEDIA

FOURTH ESTATE · *London*

First published in Great Britain in 1991 by Fourth Estate
Limited
289 Westbourne Grove
London W11 2QA

Lay All Your Love On Me Music & lyrics: Andersson/Ulvaeus,
quoted by kind permission of Bocu Music Ltd, 1 Wyndham
Yard, London W1H 1AR
Ma Baker Music & lyrics: Frank Farian/George Reyam/Fred Jay
© 1977 by Far Musikverlag GmbH, Berlin; *Rasputin* Music &
lyrics: Frank Farian/George Reyam/Fred Jay © 1978 by Far
Musikverlag GmbH, Berlin. Quoted by kind permission.

Photos supplied by:
Press Association/Topham
The Camera Press
Rex Features
The Hulton Deutsch Collection
Stills Press Agency

A catalogue record for this book is available from the British
Library

ISBN 1-85702-045-6

Designed by Bradbury and Williams
Assisted by Graham Curd

Printed in Great Britain by The Bath Press, Bath

FOREWORD

'A little knowledge is a Dangerous Thing'
Alexander Pope.

Well, I don't know about that. A little knowledge can get you on to the Gold Run on *Blockbusters*, and if you're trying to tell me Alexander Pope is more worth listening to than Bob Holness, then you've got another thing coming. Bob Holness could have Pope easily. Bob Holness could easily take out any eighteenth-century poet you care to name. Come to think of it, very very little knowledge isn't dangerous either — that could get you a fortnight in Florida on *Every Second Counts* or *Bob's Full House*. So a little knowledge is an excellent thing. Is that enough?

Professor Willard J. Bowen, Chief Editor

PREFACE

This preface is designed to assist the Reader in using this book. The Reader will find that the entries in the book are arranged in alphabetical order, and that therefore the Reader should work out which letter he or she wishes to look up, and then turn the page of the book until they find other words beginning with the same letter, and then concentrate their search down page by page until they discover the thing they are looking for. Professor Willard J. Bowen is not, by the way, Chief Editor at all. He has never seen *The Mary Whitehouse Experience*; indeed, his television cannot even pick up BBC2, since it was made in 1954 and last got a decent picture during *Maigret*.

INTRODUCTION

Hello.

PREFACE TO THE
SECOND EDITION

Shit. I knew we should have printed more books for the first edition.

FRONTISPIECE

The following initials mean that
these people take particular responsibility
for the preceding entry:

(R) Rob Newman
(D) David Baddiel
(S) Steve Punt
(H) Hugh Dennis
(A) Alvin Stardust
(K) Evil Knievel
(B) Big Johnny Holmes
(E) Eddie Hapgood
of Arsenal and England
(M) Mark Coardner out of Ride
(AH) Anoushka Hempel
(C) Henry Kelly

PROLOGUE

Now you're just pissing about. Get on with it.

Aaagh! Noise made by people when they get shot or something nasty happens to them. Hence the full Quarto text of Shakespeare's *Julius Caesar* :

CAESAR. Et tu, Brute? Aaaaagh!

Aardvark Crappy companies always call themselves something like Aardvark Double Glazing Ltd. in an attempt to be first in the phone book. As if being first in the phone book helps anyone. Possibly, in the event of getting several very similar estimates for double glazing, you might use the position of the company in the phone book as a sort of tie-breaker; but this is unlikely.

Abba Pop group famous in the 1970s. Achieved prominence in 1974 after winning the Eurovision Song Contest with 'Waterloo', a song famous for being the only Eurovision Song Contest winner not to be complete shit. Abba's four members were Agnetha (blonde and gave you the horn), Frida (brunette and not-as-obviously-horny-as-Agnetha-but-you-might-go-for-her-to-be-different), and Benny and Bjorn

(Beard. Abba's horniness-factor was distinctly male-orientated). Hits included 'Mama Mia', 'Dancing Queen' and a host of other hits you used to hate, but now quite like. Because they were Swedish, Abba's lyrics were sometimes a bit dodgy in English. For example, in 'Lay All Your Love on Me' we find the lines

> *...I'm possessive, it isn't nice*
> *You've heard me saying that smoking was*
> *my only vice*
> *Well, now it isn't true.*

Marvellous.

Abba; The defeat of Napoleon at Waterloo in 1815 inspired the Swedish songsters

Abbott and Costello Comedy double-act who made many films. Russ Abbott later got his own series on BBC1, while Costello released a string of pop hits including 'Oliver's Army', 'Shipbuilding' and 'From a Whisper to a Scream'.

Abrakebabra Ingenious name of kebab shop on the Kilburn High Road. What it's doing, you see, is blending the word 'Abracadabra' with the word 'Kebab'. Not just a very clever idea in itself, this also I think carries a subconscious suggestion that the kebabs on sale are magic.[1] (D)

---

[1]However, within three weeks, the name of this shop had been changed to 'Kebab-Araz'. What kind of pun is that?

Absolom and Achitophel Epic poem by John Dryden. It records the career of Absolom and Achitophel, a seventeenth-century comedy double-act whose career spanned the Protectorate and the Restoration of King Charles II. Their most famous routine, in which Oliver Cromwell attempted to get a refund on a dead parrot, is mentioned by Vanbrugh in *All's A Tizzy*.

Acne Nature's way of making sure that, in spite of the appalling ache in your loins that lasts for the whole of adolescence, no one will fancy you.

Action Man A doll for boys. Action Man was like Sindy or Barbie in that he possessed no secondary sexual characteristics whatsoever. Despite the advent of Real Hair in 1973, his pubic region was totally bald and he had no willy. Also, neither Sindy nor Barbie had any nipples, but their owners used to draw them on with a pink felt-tip pen (*See* CHILDHOOD PERVERSIONS).

Adolescence The period of life when boys have to master the technique of walking with their bag in front of their crotch whilst getting off the bus, so that other passengers don't see the involuntary erection inspired by the sight of a girl on the top deck. (In two-person operated buses this can be produced by the sight of a female conductor, or in extreme cases, sitting on a warm seat recently vacated by an old lady.) During adolescence boys will also worry about whether they are the Messiah, believe they have a terminal illness and, in extreme cases, think that Marillion are a good band.

Aer Lingus Comedy airline. Often used in a crap joke about it merging with Continental Airlines to form Conilingus – which is funny because it sounds like cunnilingus (a rude word).

Aftershave An excuse for men to wear perfume. Shaving is, of course, absolutely horrible, but rubbing some overpriced smelly stuff into the freshly-scraped skin makes it feel more sophisticated. No one ever buys aftershave; it always arrives at Christmas, usually from an aunt. There are two sorts of aftershave – the poncey

AFTERSHAVE: a typically subtle TV commercial

ones, and the mass-market ones. You can tell these apart because poncey ones have their advertising slogan in *French,* whereas the mass-market ones have their slogan in *English,* viz.

Denim	*For men who don't have to try too hard*
Hai Karate	*Drives women wild*
Pagan Man	*Brings out the pagan in you*
Accountant	*Pour l'homme d'Edgware*

If you are lucky these may even come in a special Christmas gift box, complete with talc, and flannel embroidered with the logo. Mmmm – that is nice.

Aga One up from the camp fire. The Aga is the least sophisticated cooker known to man. You put coal in it, set fire to the coal and the whole thing heats up. The Aga is none the less extremely posh. It is bought by two types of people.

1. Those who operate on the principle that *if it's old it must be good*; i.e. people who like the Queen Mother, people who have never driven the Morris Marina.
2. People who want a farmhouse kitchen even though they live in a 1930s semi in Edgware (*See* EDGWARE), i.e. sad people, people who watch too much *Emmerdale.*

Aga Khan Top of the range. Not only cooks, but also owns racehorses.

Agrippa Some Roman bloke. Or it may have been a woman.

Alba A superb state of the art stereo system.

All-Seater Stadium Post-Hillsborough safety idea and bollocks. There's a billion yen worth of seats at Wembley already, but as soon as

Tottenham come out, everyone's on their feet for the rest of the game, as they should be. The only difference is that in the event of a fire you now escape via 300 rows of uphill hurdles. *News at Ten* 1998: 'following a blaze at the FA Cup final, the only survivors have been named as Mr Alan Pascoe and Miss Judy Livermore.' (R)

Alpaca Type of woolly animal, probably from South America or somewhere. In zoological terms, its principal feature is that it looks ridiculous.

The Alpaca; Four-times winner of the award for World's Most Stupid-Looking Animal

Anchor Type of butter. Its advert has cows that appear to be dancing, but are in fact subjected to a very sophisticated video-editing treatment on a computer system known as Harry. Not to be confused with Country Life butter, whose advert went 'oh, you'll never put a better bit of butter on your knife', or with Lurpak, whose advert had a cow in it, but it didn't dance.

Anderson, Clive Barrister. TV host. And soon, slaphead.

Anderson, Gerry Creator of *Thunderbirds, Joe 90, Captain Scarlet, UFO, Terrahawks, Crystal Tipps and Alistair,* etc. If you want to annoy him, write a serious letter to him asking to know if Lady Penelope really insured her car with Swinton.

Animals, Running at The best way of doing this is very fast going, 'RAAAAAAAA!!!!'

CHICKENS

All the hens scarper immediately, but the cock, who will have been strutting around like a pompous git all day, will stand his ground for an extra two seconds sticking out his chest in a kind of 'Protector of the Roost' sort of way. Then, when you're about two yards away, he will quite visibly think 'Oh shit' and leg it.

SHEEP

The whole herd will bottle before you're anywhere near them, but, as they can't run very fast, you can soon overtake them, and then laugh as the stupid sheep carry on running after you.

FISH

A bit difficult as water tends to get in the way. (D)

Ant The thing about ants is that people are always going on about how chuffing brilliant they are. 'Oh their community is so socially regulated,' says Sir David La-Di-Da Attenborough (*See* ATTENBOROUGH, SIR DAVID LA-DI-DA). Not if you pour boiling water into it, it isn't. What you do is you put the kettle on and then quick smart when it's boiled, you pour it down the cracks in your patio, and before you know it all the ants come out either dead or about to die.

The next day, the surviving ants may well have

built some form of mud/dust protective barrier into the cracks. A remarkable feat of architectural engineering, this is entirely un-boiling water resistant. (D)

Aorta Vital heart organ that should not be confused with 'Atora', a sort of suet pudding heavily advertised in the 1970s. 'Atora – you're getting warmer!' It isn't that (*See* ATORA). (D/R)

Aphid What Alan Titchmarsh would talk about if you asked him round to dinner.

Apple A small, round fruit used to decorate people's fruit bowls. They last about two months before they go brown, and you have to buy some more. Mothers invariably put one in their child's packed lunch to be healthy and the kids never eat them. They eat the sandwiches, the packet of crisps and the Penguin biscuit and throw the apple at one of their friends (*See* CRAP PRANKS). Varieties include Granny Smiths, Golden Delicious, Starking, and Russet, but they all taste much the same, and they all go brown after two months. (Quicker in hot weather.)

Traditionally, 'an apple a day keeps the doctor away', but there is little evidence to suggest that any trained medical practioner would be deterred from visiting by the presence of soft fruit. In actual fact, an apple a day will probably lead to a steady build-up of pesticide residue and wax polish in the stomach unless you wash them properly. Apples are also supposed to be good for the teeth, but actually they're highly acidic, so that's also bollocks (to quote the Dept. of Health's 1987 Report *The Dental Benefits of Apples: A Myth Exploded*). However, they are used to make cider, which is excellent for getting pissed fast.

Aqueduct Like a viaduct, but instead of trains, you put water over it. The Romans built them

The ant　　　　　　　**The boiled ant**

to get water into their cities, which just proves that the Romans weren't actually as clever as historians make out, because otherwise a) they wouldn't have built cities where there wasn't any water, and b) they'd have invented pipes, rather than building bloody great aqueducts with the water out in the open air where it could evaporate in the hot Italian sun. Also ducks and stuff could swim in it and that's not very hygienic, is it?

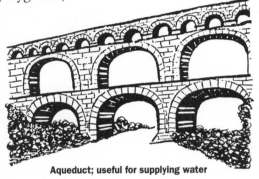

Aqueduct; useful for supplying water

Art Deco All that 1930s furniture and stuff which makes up for the lack of plot in *Poirot*.

Art Garfunkel The second most talented member of 1960s singing duo Simon and Garfunkel, he was responsible for none of their hits. He had a Number One record by himself, 'Brighteyes' – but that was about rabbits, so it doesn't count.

Arthur Film with Dudley Moore. Notable for the line 'I'm going to have another drink. Do you want another fish?' which is like really funny when you see it.

Arthur An early king of the Britons. The Arthurian legend has become a mainstay of British folk culture – there are surely few who do not know of the pulling of the sword from the stone, of the great wizard Merlin, or the deeds of the knights of Arthur's court. In spite of this there still remain severe question marks over the greatness that should be ascribed to this early leader. In the main these doubts revolve

around the following:

1. He was called Arthur.
2. This probably got shortened to Art, so he would have been King Art.
3. He had mates called Gawain, Percival and Lancelot, the last of whom ran off with his bird.
4. He was by implication responsible for 'Roundtable' on Radio One.

Arthur 2 – On The Rocks Another film with Dudley Moore. Halliwell's *Film Guide* describes it as 'shit'. Or that's the gist. It has Liza Minelli in it (*See* PEOPLE WHO ARE FAMOUS AND YOU CAN'T WORK OUT WHY).

Anwar Sadat

Artichoke Looks like a cactus but is a lot more tasty. Very embarrassing if you don't know how to eat it. The correct method is to peel off the leaves one by one, dip them in vinaigrette sauce and then scrape off the fleshy bit by dragging the leaf through your teeth. Presumably this was all worked out by trial and error after a lot of Neolithic artichoke eaters had speared themselves with the pointed bits or something (*See* FOOD, HOW MANY PEOPLE DIED TRYING TO WORK OUT WHICH BITS WEREN'T POISONOUS OR SPIKY). Anyway just as you are beginning to think that this is a piece of piss, you run out of leaves and are confronted by a large green furry ball. This is the artichoke heart. Can't quite remember how you eat this bit. Fortunately, artichokes are so posh you don't come across them very often.

McDonald's have no plans to introduce the McArtichoke.

Askey, Arthur Comedian with no legs, now dead.

Arthur Askey

Aspel, Michael Having decided to call their junior TV clips show 'Ask Aspel', the BBC had to hunt high and low to find someone called Aspel to present it. They found him in Aspel McKenna, a sheep-farmer from Kircudbrightshire, but Michael Aspel got the job, proving once again that it's not what you know, but whether you're a professional broadcaster and not a sheep-farmer.

Aston Villa Most prominent supporter – Nigel Kennedy. Every Saturday he's at Villa Park shouting, 'Come on Athton Villeh yeh monster!!' until someone beats him up.

Astrology A belief in astrology is based on two premises:

1. That a small handful of the infinite number

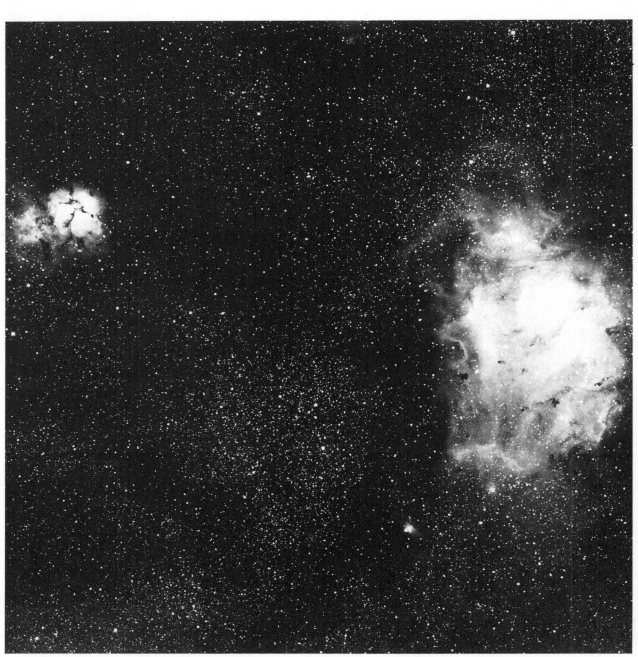

Astrology; a supernova in a distant galaxy. So watch out for a surprise visit from a relative and try not to take a financial risk until Thursday

of gravitational masses of cosmic gas, billions of light years away across the universe, exert a direct influence on the lives and financial opportunities of one of the 50 million species of carbon-based life forms on one planet, in one solar system, in one galaxy.

2. That the best person to interpret the effects is Russell Grant.

The case against astrology seems formidable. For example, six national dailies print predictions for each starsign and all six are completely different. Still, Nancy Reagan believed in it, so it must be true.

Astronomy None of us knows very much about this, but here's what it says in the *Britannica*:

> **ASTRONOMY is the science which deals with the bodies of the universe and in particular with their positions, motions, constitutions and evolution.**
>
> **THE SCOPE OF ASTRONOMY**
>
> **All astronomical observations depend on the light which reaches the earth from the various bodies. First of all the directions as seen from the earth are determined. Once the shape and size of the earth are determined, the distances of exterior bodies can be determined by methods of triangulation similar to those used in survey operations of inaccessible objects on the earth.** *Oh God. Who cares? Don't you just know that all the time he was writing this, his wife was upstairs thrusting a dildo the size of Stella-Peggiore-Major into her famished vagina.*

Ataturk, Kemal Turkish leader, so called so that whenever anyone said his name it would sound like they were patting him on the back for being a Turk: 'Ataturk!' (D)

Atora Sort of suet pudding heavily advertised in

the 1970s that should not be confused with a vital heart organ. 'Your aorta'. It isn't that.

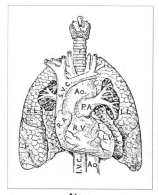 

Atora   Aorta

Should also not be confused with *Tora, Tora, Tora*, the film about the Japanese attack on Pearl Harbor named after the cry of the Kamikaze pilots; although there is also a film called *Atora, Atora, Atora!* about the one squadron of Kamikaze pilots who got it wrong and went to their deaths shouting, 'Suet pudding, suet pudding, suet pudding'. (D)

Attack on Pearl Harbor   Atora

Attenborough, Sir David La-Di-Da Bloke on TV who goes on about how bloody great animals are all the time. He forgets that it wasn't an animal who invented the TV or the safari suit. (D)

Austin The principal marque of British Leyland. The company was responsible for almost all the cars that old people drive out into the country on Sunday afternoons. When you finally reach the front of that fifteen-mile tailback, and get your chance to overtake the car that is causing it, you will find that it contains four pensioners (at least one of which is wearing a hat) and is one of the following models:

AUSTIN ALLEGRO

The flagship family car of the British motor industry during its darkest days. The original model had an oval steering wheel, which was just *rubbish*. I mean to say – *an oval steering wheel*. At its most pathetic in the sports model, which could still be burnt up by a milk float. There was a posh model, the Allegro Van Den Plas. It wasn't fooling anyone, though.

AUSTIN PRINCESS

The most upmarket Austin. Looked like a wedge of cheese on wheels and was designed to compete with the most luxuriously engineered of its continental counterparts. Somehow it seemed to miss this market and sold instead to people who liked to spend a lot of their time having their car repaired.

AUSTIN 1100

The biggest seller, its appeal was its no-frills engineering and the abundance of storage space for the inevitable tartan car blanket.

AUSTIN MAXI

Possibly the least stylish vehicle ever to grace British roads, it looked like the kind of car that you built out of Lego when you were seven, but wasn't quite as well built. The name was a clever play-on-words – *Maxi* being the opposite of *Mini,* and the Austin Mini being one of the most successful, seminal and ground-breaking cars of the era. The Maxi was, true to its name, the opposite.

Avis Car rental company whose advert said 'We

Try Harder', although how you can try harder to rent someone a car is a bit of a mystery. If someone says 'rent me a car', you can either do it or you can't.

Ayds A type of slimming biscuit you used to be able to buy in Boots, but which has now mysteriously disappeared from our shelves. No one can quite puzzle out why.

AUSTIN 1100: The self-assembly version

B

Baccarra Female singing duo of the late 1970s, now well overdue for re-release. Baccarra was Spain's revenge for Sylvia's 'Y Viva Espana'. They had two hits – 'Yes, Sir, I Can Boogie' and the even more marvellous 'Sorry I'm a Lady' which rhymed 'dynamite' with 'have you got a light'.

Backpack Travel Bores These are the people who when you ask them 'How was your holiday?' will always reply 'I haven't been on holiday, I've been travelling.' Something that you should probably have guessed from the fact that they are in BTB regulation clothing – an authentic peasant poncho, a pair of traditional goat skin Indian Sandals, and the raffia shirt of a little known hill tribe – all bought from the airport on the way back. Nor are they satisfied with the conventional two weeks, these people go for months, which is not really long enough considering how boring they are when they get back.

The first prerequisite of the BTB is that they will always have had an *amazing time*. However not all the other phrases that they habitually use to describe their exploits are as readily comprehensible:

'I was in Ethiopia during the fighting. In fact I actually spent two weeks with the Eritreans and helped them capture four Soviet rocket launchers.'

'I once changed planes in Addis Ababa.'

'Oh God, right yeah, going out of Turkey I was really bricking it at the airport because I was carrying so much stuff.'

'In my back pocket I had a nearly full packet of Anadin.'

'I really lived like a native.'

'I got bilharzia, beri-beri and spent four months on the toilet.'

'I came face to face with one of the most poisonous snakes in the world.'

'In Sydney Zoo.'

'When I was hitching in Japan I got a job for a while, but hey it's a completely different culture.'

'I spent two weeks working in Yokohama McDonald's.'

'It's completely changed me as a person.'

'I now have recurrent malaria.'

'I hit rock bottom in Borneo – no money, no food – you really find out who you are. You know what I mean.'

'I phoned my father and asked him to send me another cheque.'

Baddiel, David Lionel Member of *The Mary Whitehouse Experience* (well, I say member – for many people Baddiel surely *is The Mary Whitehouse Experience*).

Born in 1971, the illegitimate son of Bertrand Russell and Virginia Woolf, Baddiel was, by the age of seven months, already considered by many members of the Bloomsbury Set to be a new E.M. Forster, although without the poofiness. In 1974, while still at kindergarten, Baddiel wrote his first novel, *Idols of Perversity*, of which Frank Kermode said in the *Times Literary Supplement*, 'On the one hand, a sweeping satirical assault on modern values, this is also a hugely moving account of a personal pilgrimage towards self-knowledge. Perhaps he could have said a bit less about poo.' Immediately following the publication of his second novel, *Poo*, however, the now five-year-old Baddiel shocked the literary establishment by declaring a revolutionary cure for cancer, the outcome of two years' secret research at the University of Minnesota. Although the excitement surrounding Baddiel's cure is now known to have been premature – later studies having shown that 95 per cent of the treatment drug Baddielophyllin was, in fact, poo – it has now been definitely proved that all subjects used in the testing of the drug would have died anyway (probably).

It was not until he was ten, however, that the overriding fact of David Baddiel's destiny became clear: that he could have been a professional footballer (if he'd wanted to). An amazing footballer even at primary school, his distinctive playing style combining the grace of Maradonna with the vision of De Stefano, he none the less had to suffer always being picked last when teams lined up in the playground – an indictment, if ever there was one, of the much-decried tradition in English football selection of forsaking flair for mediocrity. Despite the short-sightedness of those captains (notably Simon Fund), Baddiel was still spotted by Carlos Dupiaza, Real Madrid's talent scout, on one of his regular trips to the North West London Jewish Day School's playground. Dupiaza offered him an immediate next season position playing up front

with Gunther Netzer, and the rest, as they say, is history – insofar as Baddiel said no, he had to go home, and started crying.[1]

The teenage years 1978–82 were marked by an almost unearthly sexual prowess. Having lost his virginity well before the age of puberty (the contented look on the face of the midwife who delivered him was not lost on the large crowd who had gathered outside the hospital), the onset of sexual maturity resulted in a string of highly-charged relationships between the ages of thirteen and sixteen. Marilyn Monroe, Jayne Mansfield, Golda Meir and Bronwen from *Neighbours* have all described the time they spent with Baddiel, although emotionally exhausting, as the most satisfying of their erotic life (See FRENCH, ANDY). This period is perhaps best charted in Baddiel's third novel, *I've Got An Enormous Packet*.

The decision to go to university at the age of sixteen was an unusual one, since he already held honorary degrees from the universities of Oxford, Cambridge, Harvard, Tokyo, Budapest and Malawi, but, as the character of Bavid Daddiel puts it in *Not My Life, Honest*, 'University. Hmm. That might be a good place for totty.' A similar pattern to his earlier life soon took hold. Two weeks after his arrival at King's College Cambridge, he was made Provost. In 1985 he won the Oxford and Cambridge boat-race by beating both crews single-handedly. A new college, Baddiel College, was established in his honour. Harry Porter, the archivist of the Footlights since 1887, described him as 'funnier than Peter Cook, John Cleese, Clive James, Stephen Fry and Roger de Courcy put together'.

And it was comedy, of course, that Baddiel was finally to put his well-worn muse to as a career. Having rejected offers to host *The Late Show*,

---

[1] There is no truth in the rumour, circulated in the local press at the time, confusing Carlos Dupiaza with Ted Harginty, the notorious child-abuser of North London.

Question Time, *Panorama* and *Screen Test*, he charitably decided to help out the careers of Steve Punt and Hugh Dennis (then languishing on *The Thames Help Roadshow*), and Rob Newman (then serving a ten-year jail sentence for aggravated burglary) by giving them all small cameo roles in his show, *The Mary Whitehouse Experience*. He is soon however expected to give up the programme in order to take up the post of General Secretary of the United Nations. (D)

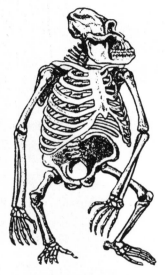

David Baddiel; Homo Kilburnus

Badger-baiting Popular sport, centred on gambling, involving the pitting of a badger against a dog, or, when the mood takes you, a car. The sport originated in 1672 in Prestwick (then capital of England), when some men discovered what a laugh it was. The most famous badger of the seventeenth century was undoubtedly 'Gentleman' Badger Badgy, although his fame was short-lived, obviously, as he got eaten by a dog. There is a softer version of badger-baiting, played on the Isle of Skye, where the badger is baited not with a dog but with irony and sarcasm. 'Call yourself a badger', 'Badgers are crap', 'You've got a smelly den', 'Go back into hibernation' and 'Is it a skunk?' are all favourite Skye-originated phrases guaranteed to put the badger's back up. (D/R)

Baghdad, Pop-up Picture of Over the page is a pop-up picture of Baghdad. (R)

Bananas Of great significance to old people, who go on and on about how there were no bananas during the war and how exciting it was when the first bananas arrived, and aren't we lucky to have bananas because during the war there weren't any at all. Oh no, it was so exciting when the first bananas arrived. Of course that's hard to believe now, but you see there weren't any bananas, well not during the war anyway. In fact there was a great shortage of bananas which meant that lots of young people, well they'd be old now I suppose, were in their twenties before they had even seen a banana, because during the war we just didn't have them you see, not one, because you just couldn't get hold of them. There's that old song 'Yes, We Have No Bananas', the very existence of which indicates that bananas were obviously pretty bloody important. Why else would you bother writing a song about them? I mean, no one's written a song called 'Sorry, We're Right Out of 4oz Bags of Frozen Peas', have they?

Banana Skins What people always fall over on in cartoons because for some reason it's funnier than falling over on anything else. Presumably they are more slippery than any other fruit skin. In real life, of course, you never even see them lying around, let alone people slipping on them. Perhaps that is partially the point.

Barbershop A form of close harmony singing which originated amongst hairdressers in the United States. The style of such songs is varied, but some of the great barbershop quartet songs include 'How Long Is It Since You Last Had This Cut Then?', 'The Last Person Who Cut This Really Didn't Know What They Were Doing,' 'I'm Leaning Over Backwards Into A Very Uncomfortable Basin (In Case A Certain

Arthur Askey receives his hospital bill.[2] (R)

Little Lady Goes By)' and 'Isn't It A Nightmare Job Being The Assistant Who Sweeps Up Hair All Day?'

Basketweaving A hobby Hugh invented for his UCCA form.

Bassey, Shirley Singer who did 'Goldfinger'. Daughter now in *Brookside*. (D)

Bastaple, Tony Former presenter of *Magpie*. A lot of posh kids weren't allowed to watch this on the grounds that it was too common, on ITV and that *Blue Peter* was on the other side. In fact your dad was just unwilling to admit that Valerie Singleton was a lot more sexy than Susan Stranks.

Bastard Term for illegitimate child. 'Oh Gods, stand up for bastards' (*King Lear*), 'No bastard shall enter the Kingdom of Heaven' (Bible, Book of Deuteronomy), 'No bastard shall enter

[2] We thought that giving a photo as well as a whole entry to the much-loved music hall entertainer may lead people to say: 'There's too much Arthur Askey', thereby echoing the immortal words of his surgeon.

after 11p.m.' (Doorman at Toppers Club, Streatham). A naughty word, but not a very naughty one, especially in the north. It's about on a level with shit in the USA (*See* ORGANIC WASTE PRODUCTS OF THE AMERICAS).

Bayeux Tapestry Tapestry in Bayeux. They didn't have any TV in 1066 so they had to record the Battle of Hastings by embroidery. Despite this apparent drawback, it's more interesting than watching *Panorama*.

BAYEUX TAPESTRY; The Normans prepare for a day out

Never pack more luggage than you need. The man furthest left has just realised he's forgotten to get any Travellers Cheques

Boulogne is a modern port, and delays are kept to a minimum

Bear, Yogi Ursine inhabitant of Jellystone National Park who had a smaller bear as his sidekick, going by the unlikely name of Booboo. This was, presumably, a nickname, so maybe he was embarrassed by his real name and didn't want the series to be called *Yogi Bear and Cedric.* Yogi Bear exhibited none of the characteristics usually associated with such animals until an incident in 1988, when he found some campers asleep in a tent, ripped their faces off and ate

On arrival at Hastings, the boats are stacked neatly on the beach. The horses are immediately attracted by the ice cream stall

The arrival of Nicholas Ridley and Bruges Group backbenchers

The Saxons get the shit kicked out of them and bottle it. William the Conqueror takes England. Shame on you, you Saxon pansies

their intestines. Police marksmen shot him with a .303 rifle, but he survived and, after surgery, accepted a $500,000 advance to turn the incident into a major film, *No More Mr Nice Guy,* which took over $12,400,000 in its opening weekend in the US.

Beardsley, Mrs Peter I heard that the reason our Kenny resigned was that the Dalglish back garden backs on to the Beardsley garden, and Mrs Beardsley was always at the fence telling Kenny who shouldn't be in the team, and who should. Mrs Peter Beardsley! Fuck, no wonder. I mean, yes, here's a woman who knows how to pick men! 'Excuse me, Mrs Beardsley, but which of your gnomes is Peter?' (R)

Beatlemania Term applied by tabloid newspapers to describe a personal appearance by any new pop band under thirty. The usual phrase is 'The crowds outside the HMV shop in Oxford Street last night were described by one policeman as "The most incredible scenes since Beatlemania."' In the last ten years there has been a most incredible scene since Beatlemania at least eight times – Haircut 100, Duran Duran, Ah-ha, Bros, Jason Donovan, New Kids on the Block, MC Hammer and Russ Abbott.

Beer Drink that tastes like sick. It is incorrect that tramps drink cleaning fluid because they can't afford beer; it's because it tastes much nicer. However, men have to keep on drinking it as the amount of beer you drink is inextricably linked to the extent of your heterosexuality. Similarly with the type of drink: drinking shandy and lager is basically a declaration of wearing women's underwear, and even Bitter is considered by many to be a prelude to going to see Duncan Norvelle. Many men, in fact, are now only happy to order a pint of cancer. (D/R)

Beethoven, Ludwig Van Never heard of him.

Bent, M. Kahn is 'M. KAHN IS BENT' was, until July 1990, painted in very large white letters on a railway bridge that crosses the North Circular road in London between Crouch End and East Finchley (just by the gasworks). It had been there for over ten years, unmissable by every single car travelling in a westward direction on the North Circular, which, bearing in mind that approximately 300,000 cars containing an average of 2.7 people pass under that bridge every day, would indicate that, over the course of that time, the fact of M. Kahn's bentness may have been impressed on 2,956,500,000 people, or round about five times the population of Europe. This kind of majority opinion must have made it very difficult for M. Kahn to dispute.

Many things, however, remain unexplained.

M. Kahn?

Considering the scale of the insult, why did the man who painted it choose to use the polite form 'M. Kahn' – as if he was writing a letter to his bank manager? Perhaps he didn't know Mr Kahn's first name (Michael? Monty?), in which case he can't have known him very well – in which case it seems a bit much to go and paint definitive statements about his sexual orientation ten feet high on the North Circular.

And perhaps even more intriguing, why was M. Kahn himself (Morry? Matt?), no doubt a resident of the Finchley area and well able to contact the local borough council, content to leave the message there for over a decade? Is it possible that he wrote it himself? Which would suggest that the graffiti was not in actual fact an insult, but the biggest sex-advert in the world. Perhaps we'll never know.

Whatever it was that persuaded the council finally to paint over 'M. KAHN IS BENT', *The Mary Whitehouse Experience* is prepared to offer a large sum of money to any person or persons prepared to go to that bridge, under cover of darkness, and paint on it the words 'M. KAHN IS STILL BENT'. (D)

Bestiality Unnatural practices with animals. The most popular animal for this purpose seems to be the sheep, judging by the number of jokes. Certainly sheep are good in bed, although they tend to be dull companions and will invariably make you pay for the cinema tickets.

Bestiality; Sheep can play hard to get

Bewes, Rodney The dull one in *The Likely Lads.*

Bible Prince Charles is always on about how the English language is falling apart, and he's probably right. There is always controversy when they bring out a new translation of the Bible. The Standard Version (1611) begins like this :

In the beginning, God created the heavens and the earth. And the earth was without form, and void; and darkness was on the face of the deep. And God said, Let there be Light; and there was light. And God saw that it was good.

Today of course, the tabloids would have phrased it differently.

GOD ALMIGHTY! LORD MAKES THE LOT

GOD, the divine being, created the universe yesterday.
He FORMED the earth and CALLED the other planets and suns into being. But everything looked a MESS! So God asked for light, and when it came, he thought it all looked GREAT! (Pictures and details, pages 4-7)

Worse than this was an attempt made in 1985 to publish an official national Bible, in a translation made by a team of civil servants.

> At the commencement and instigation God (hereinunder referred to as 'The Creator') made, formed and gave physical embodiment to the heavens and the earth (hereinunder referred to as 'The Createe'). The Createe was judged to be lacking in form and an absence of light was duly recorded on the face of the deep. The Creator then made a verbal utterance – 'Permit there to be illumination.' This measure having been implemented, the Creator expressed an opinion that, insofar as such opinion, being of itself subjective, was valid, it now all appeared satisfactory.

(N.B. The above joke – rendering an everyday statement into complex bureaucratic terms – formed the basis of four series of *Yes, Minister.*)

Of course, real traditionalists prefer the Latin version, but the BBC are not allowed to use it – 'Fiat Lux' would be advertising both a car and a type of soap.

Billy Smart's Circus The perfect excuse to turn the TV off on Christmas Day.

Birds, Flightless What is the point of a bird that can't fly? Birds are meant to fly. That is why they are called birds. What kind of a bird can't fly? A crap bird, that's what kind of bird. A bird that deserves to be extinct, that's what kind of bird. Let's face it, the dodo had it coming. How many fish can't swim? *No fish,* that's how many. In fact, the shark can't *stop* swimming, or it drowns. (Come to think of it, that's almost as crap as not being able to swim in the first place.)

So how come there are birds that can't fly? Birds that have stubby little wings, and sort of waddle around all day. Because some birds are *lazy,* that's why. Because some birds can't be bothered to get up off their arses and flap like they are meant to. We've invented the aeroplane; we're desperate to fly, but they just can't be arsed, and we've let them get away with it. We've even given penguins television commercials. It's a sad indictment of the state of our society.

Birthday, Spunky Name of pornographic film once seen by David Baddiel's brother Ivor in a gentlemen's private cinema club in the West End. Marvellous how the title allows you to infer what the plot might be. (D)

Biscuits That Sound Rude *Ginger Nuts, Hob Nobs, Macaroon* (technically a small cake, but still sounds quite rude none the less).

Biscuits, Nice

JAFFA CAKES
These are jolly tasty, even in spite of the description on the box which says '*12 light sponge cakes, with plain chocolate and a* <u>*smashing*</u> *orangey bit*'. Jaffa Cakes are nothing to do with Max Jaffa (*See* ORCHESTRA LEADERS WITH FUNNY NAMES).

Biscuits, Dull

LINCOLN BISCUITS
You can still get these although they are completely tasteless. Bought by people who think it might be interesting to have a biscuit which tastes of nothing, but has hundreds of little pimples on it. This type of biscuit is so called because it possesses strong connections with the cathedral city of the Eastern England county of Lincolnshire. Actually, the citizens of Lincoln are very proud of this, and are currently trying to twin Lincoln with other European cities which have the same names as biscuits. As you drive into Lincoln you go past a sign saying 'Welcome to Lincoln, twinned with Nice' and the Mayor is also trying to arrange a twinning with the small Bavarian town of Höbnöb.

RICH TEA

No one has yet worked out why on earth Rich Tea biscuits are so called, because if it's supposed to mean that you shouldn't eat them except with rich tea, then bollocks. I'll eat them whenever I like. And in any case, who says 'rich' tea? It's 'strong' tea. Not only a crap name, but downright wrong.

Biscuits That Are No Longer With Us

HAPPY FACES

Worked on the assumption that small children would find it more interesting to eat a biscuit if the jam on top made it look like a smiling face and that mothers would be more likely to buy them if the ad showed lots of little kids who had managed to get most of the biscuits on their faces instead of their mouths and then had a particularly ugly one smile open-mouthed at the camera while lots of jam and stuff fell out. Nice.

YO YO

A popular one for the lunch box, there were two types of Yo Yo. One in green silver foil which tasted a bit like a big After Eight and one in silver silver foil, which didn't. If you left them in your lunch box for too long they all tasted of Tupperware anyway. Called 'Yo Yo' because they always came back.

BANJO

No one is quite sure what happened to this one. It was a sort of chocolate version of the pink ones that no one eats in the Rover Biscuit Assortment. This was a thoroughly clever bit of marketing based on the assumption that if it was named after a South American musical instrument, people might suddenly begin to like a type of biscuit everyone has hated since the dawn of time (and probably before).

Black Box Loleeta Holloway's always saying 'They ripped off my vocal. It's me singing, but they got a model fronting the band, just 'cos she's young, slim and pretty.' Yes, that's right, Loleeta. And you are fat, old and ugly. I do not want to find myself sitting at home watching TV, and thinking 'Why is the housekeeper from *Tom and Jerry* on *Top of the Pops?*' You don't have time to be on *Top of the Pops* anyway: Jerry's diapered nephew is catapulting plates at Tom with a spatula fulcrum system: the kitchen will be wrecked. (R)

Boat Race, The There are many colourful, thrilling and spectacular events in the British sporting calendar. Sadly, the Boat Race is not one of them. It has been going since the mid-fourteenth century. Chaucer records in his diary for 1383 that 'todaye the talke was all of Boate Rayce; and, by heaven, 'twas all as Int'resting as a Pigge's Farte.'

As a sporting spectacle, the Boat Race fails on two counts. First, it's *a race between boats,* and all races between boats are dull, because it's either yachting, which you can only do if you're a multi-millionaire with nothing better to do (*See* CRAP POP STAR HOBBIES; SIMON LE BON*),* or it's powerboating, which you can only do if you're very, very rich but too much of a Lad to put up with going as slowly as a yacht does. The Boating Lad does not like to rely on wind-power, but instead on two Evinrude 200-hp outboards. A powerboat is, psychologically speaking, an Escort XR3i with a rudder. A powerboat driver thinks yachts are for poofs and owning a dinghy is tantamount to holding a coming-out party. Unfortunately, powerboats are crap really since you can't go anywhere in them except marinas and harbours, and also they go wrong the whole time. Whenever they show powerboat racing on TV, all the boats always break down.

The only other way you can race boats is by rowing. And that is what the Boat Race is — rowing. Rowing for speed purposes is, of course, utterly pointless in this day and age, but there is one even more crap way of propelling a boat and that is with your feet. This brings us to the pedallo (*See* UTTERLY, UTTERLY RUBBISH THINGS YOU DO ON HOLIDAY). Pedallos are only ever found bobbing about three feet offshore on Mediterranean beaches, while a group of shifty-looking criminals skulk around trying to persuade you that, rather than lie comfortably in the sun with a cold drink, you would much rather pay 400 pesetas to cycle manically around in circles and get sunburnt.

Anyway, the Boat Race. The other reason the Boat Race fails as a sporting spectacle is that it is between Oxford and Cambridge Universities, and the majority of the population are not going to spend a Saturday afternoon glued to the TV desperate to know which of the two great medieval centres of learning has rowed from one western suburb of London to another the fastest.

One would also think, given that Oxbridge students are supposed to be so bloody clever, they'd have worked out that if you want to get from Putney to Mortlake, you get the number 9 bus.

Of course, in the old days, the Boat Race was more of a draw than it is now. In the 1920s lots of undergraduates came down to London to cheer on Varsity, and by tradition, the night before, you were supposed to try and steal a policeman's helmet. It would be interesting to see this tradition revived now since the sort of Oxbridge undergraduate who is going to bother 'going to town' to watch the Boat Race is invariably going to be a wanker. If you tried to steal a policeman's helmet in the 1920s, the cheery bobby would turn round and say, 'Caught you, you whippersnapper! I don't know, these youthful high spirits. . . be off with you, sir, and God bless.' Nowadays, the constable will squirt tear gas in your eyes before truncheoning you to the ground, and quite honestly, good thing too.

BOAT RACE: Oxford's controversial tactics in 1986 led to disqualification

Bodybuilding A pastime of very sad people who think that the bigger your muscles are the more attractive you are to women, which is plain nonsense (according to D. Baddiel). All it means is that you have to buy shirts that are bigger than other people's, you have to spend a lot of time in the gym pumping iron and that, when you are old, all the muscle turns to fat and you look really crap.

Bogart Posh form of bogie. In polite company, it is not *de rigueur* to say 'Excuse me, I've got a

bogie.' It is however perfectly acceptable to say 'Excuse me, I've got a bogart.' In fact, if you use 'bogart', it is then even acceptable to wipe it under the table. (D/R)

Bogie Well, we all know what this is, but, inter-estingly, it's one of those kids' words which also refer to something proper – in this case, a type of attachment on a train. This means that at top-level board meetings to discuss the design of new trains like the Intercity High Speed Chunnel 125, someone at some point has to say

BATTLE OF THERMOPYLAE: The Athenians go two lengths up

'I think we should put a large bogie on it' and everyone there has to nod and pretend that they can't think of anything else that bogie means. Although this doesn't explain why the Intercity High Speed Chunnel 125 is actually described in BR's planning leaflet as 'incorporating a ten-foot piece of mucus, one side of which is crusty, but one side of which is almost liquid.' (D/R)

Boney M Marvellous. It's hard to believe nowadays, but in the late 1970s Boney M were incredibly popular. Like Abba, they were foreign but wrote their lyrics in English. This did not stop them from picking very highbrow, historical subjects for their songs. Their first major UK hit, 'Ma Baker', took as its theme a real-life gangster from 1920s Chicago:

> *Ma Baker!*
> *She taught her four sons*
> *Ma Baker!*
> *To handle their guns.*

But their acknowledged masterpiece was 'Rasputin', telling the story of the legendary 'mad monk' of pre-Revolutionary Russia. The chorus went

> *Ra ra Rasputin*
> *Lover of the Russian queen*
> *There was a cat that really was gone!*
> *Ra ra Rasputin,*
> *Russia's greatest love machine*
> *It was a shame how he carried on.*

This view proved highly influential among world historians. See A.J.P. Taylor's *Real Gone Cat: Late Czarist Russia and the Rise of Bolshevism,* and the new BBC2 8-part documentary, *It Was a Shame How They Carried On.*

Boredom A condition often suffered by the super-intelligent, i.e. Rob Newman and David Baddiel. You know how if you're not super-intelligent, you might get bored with a Nintendo Game Boy after about twelve days; that's how we felt after about twelve days on the planet. It simply can't offer us all much. What is there, really? Sex, a few books, the odd early episode of *Oh No, It's Selwyn Froggit.* (R/D)

Boss Cat The thing about *Boss Cat* was, it was only called *Boss Cat* in Britain, because the BBC thought it would be advertising Top Cat cat food to call it by its real title, which was, of course, *Top Cat.* This is why, all the way through, everybody was referring to the central character as *T.C.* and not *B.C.* (who later became a cartoon character in his own right). It is very hard to see why the BBC was so worked up about this, since the average *Top Cat* viewer was about nine years old, and the purchasing power of nine year olds in the pet-food market is minimal. Perhaps the BBC thought that millions of brainwashed nine year olds would be forcing their mothers down to the supermarket to buy Top Cat cat food unless they prevented this by the clever means of putting the words 'Boss Cat' over a song that clearly went

> *Top Cat! the most respectable*
> *Top Cat! whose intellectual*
> *Close friends get to call him T.C.*
> *Providing it's with dignity. . .*

Actually, of course, the problem was that you couldn't hear the words. It always sounded like the song went

> *Top Cat! The mossesseptable*
> *Top Cat! Whose into let you all*
> *Close friends get to call him T.C.*
> *Pro-Fighting is whipped in the tea.*

That's how I thought it went, anyway. Another interesting thing about *Top Cat* was that most of its jokes were way over the heads of its audience. Trouble was, though, that it used to have that crap canned laughter all over it that Hanna-Barbera use to make all their cartoons sound like an episode of *Joint Account*.

Bouncers There's no distress-restrictions when a bouncer – a bouncer – decides that I, with my table-talk the toast of dinner-parties from Gstaad to Boston, and with my swanky garments on, can't get into the Birmingham Dome without a bit of grief and hassle first.

It is, however, an irony at which I've learnt to laugh and can even share pleasantly with the bouncers, too. 'Doesn't it strike you as absurd, footman, the idea of you arbitrating over other people? I mean excuse me, but don't you spend all Saturday afternoon in a vest, chain-smoking in our kitchen with a Cortina on bricks outside, reading last week's *Sun Day* and looking at your watch. Six hours till you put on the DJ – a garment, incidentally, which the rest of the race wears for weddings and Nobel Prize collections, and you wear for manslaughter, you Cro-Magnon throwback.' Six more hours and you can take out all that Neanderthal resentment of a species that leaves you standing on the cold threshold, and goes off into their Bronze Age world of music, dyed clothes and talk of Glastonbury and Stonehenge. (R)

Bowie, David Made self-obsession acceptable, and ruined a million adolescent conversations. (R)

Bowyer, Ernie Rob's Grandpop. Worked at Smithfield Meat Market and considered himself a Tory because the Duke of Kent once came and shook hands with all the stallholders. Also because he earned 2s/6d a week (although this was 1982). Refused to place any of his reputed three-figure savings in the Bradford & Bingley building society on the grounds that they were

'a couple of jokers'. (R/D)

Boxing Sport where people hit each other.

ORIGINS

Before the 8th Marquess of Queensberry invented a set of rules for it, boxing was known simply as 'fighting' (*See* FIGHTING, HARDNESS). It's quite surprising that boxing was invented by the 8th Marquess of Queensberry, as it has to be assumed from his name that he was a bit of a poof (*See* NAMES, POOFY). However, it is quite possible that because he had a poofy name, he was constantly getting into fights in response to people shouting 'He's bald, he's bent, his arse is up for rent, he's the Marquess of Queensberry'. Alternatively, 'Marquess of Queensberry' may simply have been nineteenth-century-speak for 'Captain of Queensberry'. The Queensberry rules, drawn up in 1879, govern boxing to this very day. Here they are:

1. Each boxer's entitle must be accompanied by a rousing soul number (e.g. 'The Only Way Is Up' by Yazz) or a rap you've done yourself.

2. On this entitle, each boxer must wear a silk dressing-gown with a hood and his name written on the back. Any boxer who enters wearing a blue towelling number given away free with a 200ml pack of Dunhill Aftershave should be immediately docked *five* points.

3. In interviews, every boxer must have some sort of weird slightly effeminate speech defect or lisp.

4. In between rounds, there must be a bit of crumpet in a spangly leotard carrying round the number of the next round on a large card above her head;

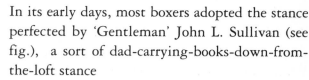

In its early days, most boxers adopted the stance perfected by 'Gentleman' John L. Sullivan (see fig.), a sort of dad-carrying-books-down-from-the-loft stance

In fact, the John L. Sullivan stance, as is perhaps obvious, is a very bad and spacky way to hold your fists in order to fight somebody and John L. Sullivan himself would probably not have been world champion for twenty-eight years had most of the other boxers *not* adopted the John L. Sullivan stance.

CHRIS EUBANK

The first thing that needs to be said about Chris Eubank is that his second name is Eubank. Now we know what most people think about when they hear the word 'Eubank', but in actual fact it derives from the old Saxon word *'Eubanke'*, which meant 'non-electronic carpet sweeper'. Something is clearly wrong here because surely boxers should not be named after domestic household items. It takes something away from the event to go to a match and hear the referee announce, 'And in the blue corner, weighing in at two hundred and ninety pounds, Mike Kenwood Chef!!!' or 'And in the red corner, the WBO undisputed cruiserweight champion of the world, Sugar Ray J-Cloth!!!'

CRUELTY

When Chris Eubank beat Nigel Benn to take the middleweight championship, the anti-boxing lobby gained a lot of ground, because there was no doubt that there was someone in the ring that night who could be described as the most sadistic and cruel beast ever seen on television – ITV interviewer Gary Newbon. Nigel Benn was crying, had apparently lost an eye, and was about to retire on the spot, when Gary offered him this word of comfort: 'Well, Nigel – you've just seen all your dreams fly out the window.'

'Well Jackie - you've just seen your husband's brains fly out of the window.'

Dallas 1963: Gary Newbon begins his illustrious career of on-the-spot TV journalism.

Chris Eubank, meanwhile, was saying: 'I'm in excruciating pain. I think I've split my tongue open. I need to go to hospital.' Gary's response was: 'So, Chris – you must be feeling on top of the world.'

Britain, Regional Geography Of In spite of their small size the British Isles have immense regional diversity in both their landscape and people, who none the less live in great harmony with each other. However certain offensive stereotypes may still be found:

SCOUSERS

From the great port city of Liverpool in the north-west of the country, all Scousers are natural comedians. Be careful what you say to them as they will certainly counter with an example of their honest and hard-edged wit. You can, of course, riposte in the traditional manner: 'Fuck Off, you Scouse Bastard.'

COCKNEYS

All cockneys are natural street traders never more at home than when flogging mouldy Espana Oranges, or dodgy electrical equipment. Easily recognisable by their charming sales banter, the speed with which they disappear whenever they spot a policeman and the fact that everything you buy from them falls apart as soon as you get it home. Their undisguised belief that London is the only decent place in Britain plus the fact that most of them support Arsenal (*See* ARSENAL, but only if there are no other matches on) makes them extremely popular.

GEORDIES

All Geordies are naturally rugged (*See* BEWES, RODNEY) and say 'pet' a lot. They like building ships. Paul Gascoigne is a Geordie, and apparently the fog on the Tyne is all his, although quite why anyone would want the fog on the Tyne no one knows. Sounds like his agent's negotiated a bad deal for him there. 'Your fee for opening this supermarket, Paul, will be. . . some fog.'

British Empire The British have always been a nation of seafarers and it did not take long for the inhabitants of these plucky little islands to covet other lands beyond the seas. Much of the Empire was built up through discovery and colonisation of virgin lands, but the majority of it was stolen from other European powers who were by no means as hard as we were and who had no bottle when confronted by the thin red line. The first possession of the Empire was somewhat disappointing being a useless lump of rock off the east coast of Canada. Imaginatively this was called Newfoundland on the basis that they had newly found it. From then on acquisitions continued apace until at its height one quarter of the world's population owed allegiance to the British Crown.

So large was the area covered that, by the start of the twentieth century, our colonial administrators could claim that the sun never set on the Empire, for as soon as night fell in its westernmost domain the sun would rise in its easternmost. If this indeed was the aim of our Empire building there were surely cheaper alternatives than the massive feats of administration that this global Empire required. The Norwegians, for example, restricted their empire to Lapland, on which they could claim that the sun did set, but only for ten minutes a night. Furthermore, as no one lived there, their costs were kept low. In place of the huge standing army the British required to maintain India, all the Norwegians required was a couple of willing volunteers, two parkas and several pairs of snow shoes. Indeed, so expensive was the Empire that, as soon as it

had been accumulated, it had to be relinquished. But even here mistakes were made. The French, for example, gave up everywhere except those places it would be nice to go on holiday, and therefore retain the Caribbean islands of Martinique and Guadeloupe. The British, by contrast, gave up everything except the Falkland islands, which are no use to anyone unless you are in a state of extreme sexual frustration. Also, in the Caribbean, you don't find all the beaches are covered in penguins and fat, blubbery walruses. You try placing your sun-lounger among that lot.

Even today, however, remnants of Empire survive (*See* CRICKET; CURRY; CRUSTY OLD TWATS IN THE HOUSE OF LORDS WHO THINK THAT BRITAIN IS STILL IMPORTANT).

British Holidays For years British holidays have had a bad press. This was based largely on the fact that the British weather was crap and you couldn't get a suntan. However, in 1990 everyone realised that sunbathing was bad for you so they decided to stay at home, and what happened? Britain had its hottest summer for thirty years. If Britain's summers stay hot, it's bad news for Centre Parcs. Centre Parcs are holiday centres built on the assumption that the only way to enjoy a holiday in Britain is to spend it in a giant conservatory off the M1. The idea is that you avoid the rain by spending a fortnight under an all-weather dome that looks like a mutant from the garden section of the Argos catalogue. Inside there are swimming pools with waterslides and artificial gardens: in other words, it's a giant leisure centre only without the machine in the foyer (where you put the money in and watch a packet of Wotsits and a Wagon Wheel get pushed off a shelf and fall into a tray at the bottom, where you pick them up and read the words 'Best Before End October 1987').

Even today, in the age of the cheap jet charter,

certain types of holiday have remained popular in Britain:

CYCLING HOLIDAYS

The kind of people who go on cycling holidays are the kind of people who on their eleventh birthday chose a sensible bike with a basket rather than a Raleigh Chopper, and then spent their time doing their cycling proficiency test rather than wheelies in the car park of the local Sainsbury's.

WALKING HOLIDAYS

For a walking holiday you need certain things: a good map, stout shoes, waterproof clothing and most importantly of all, a beard. No one is quite sure why all walkers have a beard — it may provide extra storage space when the rucksack is full. Sometimes of course, walkers will venture further afield and enjoy a different type of holiday. They're easy to spot — they're the only people on the beach wearing a cagoule.

Britten, Benjamin Not as famous as those other composers like Beethoven or Mozart, but he was British so he gets mentioned a lot.

Bronwen Female character until very recently in *Neighbours,* now left to marry Henry in New Zealand, although as we all know Henry's actually gone to *Home and Away.* Bronwen, or Bronny, was undoubtedly the most gorgeous woman in *Neighbours.* I mean, I accept that for a long time it was Jane. And I'm prepared to believe that Kylie Minogue looked all right in a certain light. But Bronwen was the one you'd want to shag. Now who is there? Kerry: no thank you. Sharon: I'd prefer Bouncer. Those two twins they've got in are clearly supposed to provide some sort of glamour element, but one of them's got a bit of a wonky mouth and you'd never be able to get that out of your mind even if you were actually doing it with the nicer one.

I think Helen's probably your best bet now. Obviously, she's getting on a bit, but she's got a very sexy way of finishing every single sentence in a husky whisper. And it didn't half turn me on when she had that stroke.

Actually, Madge is all right. (D)

Bruce, Robert the The first Australian king of Scotland. What a crap joke.

Brush, Basil A fox who used to have his own TV series. There were three blokes who did it with him — Mr Derek, Mr Roy and Mr Rodney. Mr Derek was actually Derek Fowldes, who is now in *Yes, Minister* (see above) and never likes to talk about how he used to co-star with a children's puppet. The best thing would be if Paul Eddington was struggling to understand one of Sir Humphrey's long polysyllabic sentences and Basil Brush popped up and said, 'You can't leave

Blast-Off Basil there Mr Derek. Ah ha ha ha, boom boom.'

'I say, Mr Roy, what do you mean we haven't got a second series?'

Brush, Bog Term for person with a particular hairstyle.

Cabbagey Smell that comes out of old people's noses. Medical opinion is divided on the reason for this. Some doctors believe that after the age of sixty, cabbage patches start sprouting in the sinuses. Others believe that senility makes pensioners eat through their noses (although this view was discredited by Dr. P.W. Jameson in his 1959 paper, *Old People Don't Just Eat Cabbage*). (D)

Cagoule, The Worn by walkers, it is traditional to cover the front of the cagoule with fabric badges of the various interesting places you have been while wearing it. Generally these are places as interesting as Harlech, Caernarvon, or various small castles on the Cleveland Way.

Cant, Brian That bloke who used to do *Playaway*. Not to be confused with Cantabrian, who make hurdles for athletics tracks.

Cantabrian Company who make hurdles for athletics tracks.

Catholicism Any assessment of Catholicism must first take in the fact that it was only two years ago, in 1989, that the Pope unofficially

pardoned Galileo for declaring that the earth goes round the sun. An extraordinary and controversial decision, this represented the most radical ecclesiastical edict since the pronouncement that the M25 goes round London, rather than, as had previously been believed under pain of death, that London goes round the M25.

Cardinal Ptolomey of Rome was the first to speak out against the Pope's rash declaration. Writing in the Catholic Church's journal, *The Purple Dress*, under the headline 'HAS THE POPE GONE STARK STARING MAD?' he asked, 'What next? The earth is round I suppose!' Later in the article, Ptolomey tempered his views slightly with the comment, 'I am not one of those who believe the Catholic Church should resist all forms of change. For some time now, for example, I've believed the name

Cardinal Ptolomey

"Mesopotamia" should be changed to "Mesopata", to mark where you fall off the edge.'

However, apparently, as part of their new efforts to mend the schism in Christianity, the Anglican Church is presently preparing to make an announcement to the effect that the Reformation never happened. The announcement will be made on BBC TV, after which viewers should understand that the flat object with the bright orange circle going around it is the BBC globe. Moreover, in keeping with the tenets of Catholic cosmological understanding – known technically as the 'Well – that's what it looks like from here' argument – all space exploration is then going to have to abide by the premise that the moon is about a hundred yards away, and that therefore Apollo 15 need only be a ladder. (R/D)

Chamberlain, Neville Pre-war Prime Minister who visited Hitler and returned with a piece of paper saying it was Peace in our Time. And how wrong he was! But, you know, it's very easy, with the benefit of hindsight, to criticise Chamberlain for failing to foresee World War Two. Far better to criticise him for being a drunk and an abuser of farm animals, because he's dead, so we can't be done for libel (*See* GOLDMAN, ALBERT*).

Chinese Cultural Revolution History's great fashion disaster. Millions of small people dressed in identical peaked-caps and blue overalls: Soyuz II reported that from space they looked like Casey Jones' sperm. (R/D)

Christmas Christmas is the time when we stuff ourselves with food and drink, and we are forced to travel hundreds of miles to see members of the family we don't even like very much. In addition to this, we send out cards with jolly messages in them:

Christmas Day

6.30am
Morning Worship
Remember the true meaning of Christmas. With Noel Edmonds and Gordon the Gopher.

7.00am
Cartoon Time
The Destructors, He-man and the Sexist Stereotypors, The Cheapoanimators and Scooby Doo.

7.30am
The Great Escape *(r)*
Towards the end of World War Two, a group of prisoners including Jim Rockford, Charles Bronson, Steve McQueen and that bloke off of *The Man from UNCLE* decide to dig a tunnel. Classic entertainment. And a bloody sight better than *The Wizard of Bleeding Oz.*

9.30am
The Noel Edmonds up the Top of the Post Office Tower Show
With guests who are giving up their Xmas morning for a huge cheque.

11.30am
Spuddy the Racoon
Heart-warming Disney feature which is immensely cheap. Suddenly you wish you had Sky Movies, don't you? Don't worry, later on there's a massive hit film we've paid millions of pounds for. Shame you've already seen it eight times on video.

12.30pm
Best of Top of the Pops 1991

12.31pm
Tom and Jerry
With Noel Edmonds.

3.00pm
The Queen
Her Majesty addresses what's left of the Commonwealth while millions of misty-eyed subjects raise their glass and solemnly say the traditional words,'What on earth is she wearing?'

3.15pm
The James Bond Film: Never Say Wasn't This One On Last Year Again

7.00pm
The Les Dennis Christmas Special

8.00pm
The Russ Abbott Christmas Special

9.00pm
Bread Christmas Special

10.00pm
Allo Allo Christmas Special

11.00pm
Panorama Christmas Special
Yuletide with the Nicaraguan Death Squads.

12.45pm
Psycho Cop Killer
Stop arguing over the Monopoly and watch a bit of gruesome death. With Noel Edmonds.

Greetings to your Family at this joyous time,
Noel to all men with this happy Christmas rhyme!
Here's a card to wish you every Yuletide cheer,
Though I couldn't give a fuck about you
All the rest of the year!

and your aunt turns up with her Rover Biscuit Assortment (a sad comedown for a once prestigious car manufacturer). It is a time when people do things that at any other time of year would get them certified. Things like eating 3lbs of walnuts at one sitting, setting fire to a steam pudding or dragging a large coniferous tree into their lounge, wedging it in a bucket with two old bricks and then covering it with small flashing lights, one of which isn't connected properly.

Above all Christmas is an orgy of television which invariably looks like the panel opposite.

Clag A word which owes its existence to design flaws in Andrex.

Class If I'm ever talking to an upper-class or an upper-middle-class woman, I just feel so unsexy. I can feel myself turning into a World War Two greengrocer: my hair flattens down into a brilliantined centre-parting, and I sprout an overall with chipped bics in the top pocket. And halfway through my rakish theory about why, say, Auden and Larkin are the acceptable face of country and western, I cave in and start saying 'I've saved you the crispy lettuce as always, young Miss Asquith, and how is Lord Asquith at the Great Manor – if I may be so bold. Trade unions? Fancy word for loafer, if you ask me. Our youngest is taking lessons in the new pianoforte, and we're hoping she might win a place at the new municipal polytechnical college I'M SO DIRTY! I'M SO DIRTY! FUCKING FUCKING FUCKING!!!' (R) (ON SECOND THOUGHTS ONE OF THE OTHERS.)

Clause 29 Clause 28 is the section of local government legislation that forbids the promotion of homosexuality. Clause 29 is the section of local government legislation that forbids the promotion of Charlton Athletic. Clause 29 was actually passed on to the legislature in 1899, when Charlton Athletic sported long shorts, peaked caps, and big, bushy moustaches – which is why it's often confused with Clause 28. (R/D)

Gunner-Sgt. Henry De Montford-Smith, Corinthians centre-half during the Challenge Cup Victory season, 1901-2.

Clay Pigeon Shooting The pigeon, once captured, is first covered in wet clay, baked in a kiln and then glazed. This hampers its ability to fly away, making it much easier to hit. Should a clay pigeon not get shot, and land intact on the ground, it can survive in the wild for up to ten minutes, assuming, that is, that it didn't die in the oven, or even from just being covered in

51

clay. Particularly as in an effort to provide a clean, rounded surface, it is necessary to grout in the little nostrils in the beak. And they call that a sport. (R/D)

Clitty, Don't Forget To Tickle My Thing said direct to camera by the heroine of *Spunky Birthday* (*See* BIRTHDAY, SPUNKY) from the back seat of her car, after her feet have been placed in the two front windows and the windows wound up. This may seem at first glance a superfluous piece of dialogue, but in fact in this sort of situation, it is quite common for the chauffeur and unspecified-moustachioed man to think: 'Right, that's that sorted', and then go and do some shopping. (R/D)

Clouds Understanding clouds can be an invaluable asset if you want to be properly dressed for the prevailing weather conditions.

Coach Travel A nightmare, but cheap. All coaches in the UK run to a strict timetable reflecting the average journey time over that route (assuming there is no other traffic, no contraflows and the coach is fitted with the thruster units from a Saturn Five). As a result the coach in which you are travelling either isn't moving at all or is careering along in the fast lane in an attempt to break Sir Malcolm Campbell's long-standing land-speed record. However horrifying the speeds attained, the coach will still arrive late.

Apart from this, coach travel is a pleasure marred only by the apple core someone has left in the ashtray in front of you, the greasy patch on the window caused by the previous occupant's unwashed hair, the small blower nozzle above your head which has two settings: 'off ' and 'Hurricane Hugo' and worst of all the fact that you have to travel 200 miles listening to

Cirrus

Cirrostratus

Nice day tomorrow

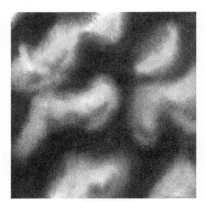
A bit shit

First day at Wimbledon

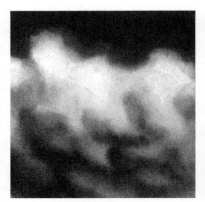
It's going to piss down

the driver's own choice of cassette. There is nothing worse than sitting in the rain on the M1 listening to *Richard Clayderman Plays House Hits.*

Computer Perhaps the most useful thing invented in the twentieth century with the exception of the Remington Fuzz-away and Nose-hair Trimmer. Computers are, in essence, binary switching devices, working on the reversed-polarity principle to perform calculations at the rate of millions per second. They also make funny noises and play games. They can be used for all sorts of tasks, such as major fraud, weapon guidance systems, or preventing you from getting a tenner out of your cashpoint machine because you're 87p overdrawn.

Many people now work with computers on an everyday basis, which is interesting since computer terminals give off ionising radiation, which causes cancer. They don't allow pregnant women to use computers, you know (*See* CIRCUMSTANTIAL GUESSWORK QUOTED BY HYPOCHONDRIACS).

Amongst the many places you will find computers are travel agents, where they have these really flash ones that can call up any flight, holiday, etc. at the touch of a button. Unfortunately the programmes to operate these are so complicated that the travel agent is usually incapable of using it. Enter any High Street travel agent and the phrase you will hear more than any other is, 'I pressed that, but it didn't do anything.'

Corduroy Type of trousers much worn by Steve Punt when he was a sixth-former, I should think. (D)

Cormack, Tim Born in Leeds in 1957 and became one of the leading rock guitarists of his generation. From an early age he shunned the conventional 'boring love songs' standard in the

pop world and searched for wider influences. In his late teens he read Jung, Schopenhauer and Freud, which led to his first album, *Clever Germans.* In 1976 released unsuccessful concept album based on the *Tibetan Book of the Dead.* In 1978 finally found success after reading *The Reader's Digest Book of Home Improvement.* After forming his own band, The Tim Cormack Band, he had an immediate hit with 'Paint Your Love on Me (In Two Coats)'. The follow up to this, 'Our House of Love is Leaking (Put Some Mastic Tape On the Roof)' went to Number One for six weeks, as did the album, *Fix Your Love to My Wall (And Use a Rawlplug).* In interviews Cormack admitted that he was 'heavily influenced' by the book, but denied that he had plagiarised it directly. His next single, 'Downpipes and Bracketing', was 'a hymn to good guttering' – *NME,* while in 1980 a visit to New York produced a harder, funkier edge and his first dance record 'Do The Black and Decker Workmate'. By now critics were lauding his success in tapping into DIY as a previously unexploited source of musical inspiration, but Cormack, ever perverse, announced his intention to 'keep moving, keep growing; an artist must never grow complacent or stale'. With this he released 'The Oil of Love (Is Draining From my Sump)' and a worldwide audience recognised that Cormack had found new inspiration, this time from *The AA Guide to Car Maintenance.* A string of hits followed, including 'The Alternator Song','Screenwash', and 'You Can't Hurry Tappet-Adjustment'. The double-album *Full Service* followed and Cormack then became a recluse, retiring to a Gloucestershire manor-house. Rumours that he was addicted to heroin were scotched when, in 1987, he suddenly re-emerged with a new single, 'The World's Highest Waterfall (Is in Venezuela)' – a song, which, like the rest of the album, was based on a 'book that changed my life' – *The Sunday Times World Atlas.* The follow-up single, 'I Didn't

Know Hungary Was There', went to Number One.

Crane, Lee The one the girls always fell for in *Voyage to the Bottom of the Sea* which was the same as all they now have on Channel 4, like *Time Tunnel* and *Land of Primitive Techniques of Superimposition*.

Cricket You either love it or you hate it. Or you may be asleep.

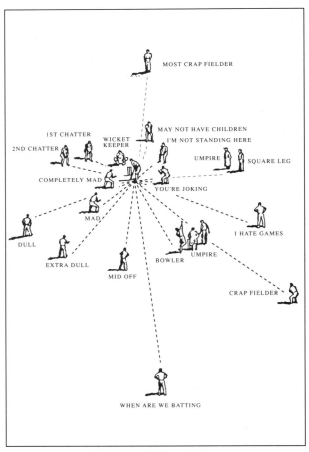

Some of the fielding positions

Curry Type of food eaten after the pubs shut. Curry comes in many forms, such as Korma, Dupiaza, Shahi, Bhuna, Biryani, etc., etc., but they all taste much the same after seven pints of lager. The thing to do when you go for a curry is

always order far too many poppadoms. You order these because you are very hungry when you arrive, but after you've eaten ten of these bastards (deep-fried greasy discs that look like huge crisps), you won't have room left for the main course, which is what you've paid the money for. What's more, the waiter knows full well that you're going to fall for this old one. Which is quite fair, as it gives him some recompense for the amount of times drunken wankers have clicked their fingers at him and said, 'Oi, Gandhi.'

The other thing to do when you go for a curry is to delegate one person at your table to be the one who says 'Actually, of course, in India they never eat anything like this.' Which is quite true, as Indians never make the mistake of ordering far too many poppadoms. Another person at your table should be the One Who Orders Egg and Chips Because They Don't Like Foreign Food (*See* WAYS YOU CAN TELL OTHER BRITISH TOURISTS WHEN ABROAD). Best of all, however, someone should make a point of ordering the hottest curry on the menu to show what a Lad they are. They will, of course, spend the rest of the meal hyperventilating, choking and burning their throat, but it is imperative that if you want to be Hard, then you don't Eat Foreign unless you can burn your mouth off. For this type of person the best type of curry is made from chunks of pit-bull terrier with chili, turmeric and nitric acid. Also you must eat it all, even if you spend the rest of the night projectile-vomiting over several miles' distance. Remember – *the Hard person does not leave any curry on his plate, not for no one.*

Cycling Proficiency Test An archaic ritual, designed in the days when traffic levels were roughly a hundredth of what they are now. The poncey manoeuvres you learn for this test are a cruel pretence that cycle-safety in the 1990s is down to anything other than sheer chance. A redesigned Cycling Proficiency Test should include exercises such as:

APPROACHING A MAJOR JUNCTION

1) Apply brakes well ahead of junction.
2) Look round to check traffic and get huge eyeful of grit.
3) Signal right.
4) Get arm knocked off by bus. Hit kerb. Breathe in several lungfuls of unburned hydrocarbons and carbon monoxide from crappy old Cortina whose brain-dead owner can't be bothered to have an MOT. Make determined effort to move to centre of lane, while 400-ton Belgian juggernaut releases airbrakes in your face. Get screamed at by obnoxious fat sales rep. in dented Sierra. Shout 'Fuck off!' vaguely in direction of blaring horns.
5) Look in both directions.
6) Wait while solid streams of traffic in both directions totally ignore you.
7) Die of old age.

Cynicism *See* BADDIEL, DAVID.

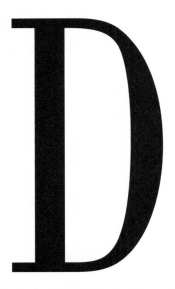

Dead Not alive. Also a Merseyside synonym for 'very', as in 'that's dead good' or 'he's dead handsome', or '*Bread* is dead unfunny.'

Death Penalty The best thing about the death penalty was that, before he could sentence someone to death, a judge had to put a small piece of black cloth on his head.[1] What with the wig and everything, this meant that a hanging judge would have a fair amount of stuff on his head. In fact, the family of John Smithers, who was sentenced to death in 1934, later complained that the solemnity of the moment was somewhat marred by the attempts of the judge to also balance on his head a glass decanter and a tomato – and then shouting 'Call Norris McWhirter . . . quickly!'

Before hanging, execution involved being beheaded by a man wearing a black mask. The use of a disguise meant that a lot of people used to assume that this man was Jeremy Beadle, which may in turn explain why all the pictures painted of Charles I's execution show him smiling, tapping his nose, and playing up to a hedge where he thought he could see a camera. And also why Lightfellow's portrait of Charles I's head in the basket shows him looking somewhat pissed off. (R/D)

Denied It, He Who Supplied It Phrase used after someone has farted to throw suspicion on any person present who refuses responsibility for the smell. It effectively makes the question 'Have you farted?' a Catch-22 situation, replies of either 'yes' or 'no' implicating the accused party equally. There is, however, an escape clause offered by the response 'He who smelt it, dealt it', or, alternatively, by the response 'Fuck off.' (D)

Dennis, Hugh Born the son of a Portuguese nobleman, he served his country with distinction in both the East Indies and Morocco establishing a reputation as a fearless and intrepid navigator. His ambitions, however, were on a far grander scale and feeling that his achievements had not been justly rewarded in his homeland he offered instead to serve the Spanish Crown. Thus it was that flying the flag of King Charles V, he set sail from the port of Seville in an attempt to find the elusive westward route to the Spice Islands and the Moluccas. The onset of a harsh and unforgiving winter forced his fleet of five vessels to seek winter quarters in a sheltered natural harbour on the South American coast. As soon as fairer weather set in however he continued his quest and, believing that he had found the westward passage to the Pacific, he set sail through the straits that now bear his name. After a stormy 360-mile passage, in which two vessels were lost and a mutiny quelled by his ruthless leadership, he finally entered the western ocean on 28 October 1520, thus becoming the first person to discover a route over which ships could sail a complete circle of the world. Oh all right – that was Magellan.

[1] This may be the reason why Geoffrey Trottman, a suspected murderer who was pardoned at the last minute in 1952, fainted when he met Terry Wogan.

Dentists' Waiting Rooms Notable for their massive selection of out of date magazines. This of course raises many questions.

1. Where do they all come from ?
2. Why are none of them ever less than a year old?
3. Has the dentist read them all? and if so, why are all dentists so dull?
4. Why are some of the colour pictures always cut out?
5. Why is there always a copy of *The Hare and Hound?*

The other thing you immediately notice about the magazines in dentists' waiting rooms is that they are all totally irrelevant to the circumstances under which they are read. Shrewd publishers have noticed a gap in the market here and are planning to bring out magazines specifically aimed at the waiting-room market, including *Which Drill?*, *Amateur Anaesthetist*, *Classic Root Canal* and *Immense Pain Quarterly*.

Deodorant A method of disguising how we are naturally meant to smell. All animals require some mechanism to cool themselves down when they get too hot. The technique however differs from animal to animal. Dogs cool down by sticking their tongues out and panting. In humans, this technique is only used by certain men who visit exclusive cinema clubs in Soho. In general humans cool down by sweating which would be a very efficient technique if it weren't for the fact that it makes all your clothes wet and it don't half stink. The sweatiest part of the body is the armpit, which is a gross design error – it's dark, it's warm and air never gets to it – if you leave sweat there it is the bodily equivalent of putting your old, wet football socks in a carrier bag on top of the boiler.

In ancient cultures such bodily odours were thought to be attractive. The sweat of the male was a major plus factor when pulling, virility often being measured by the size of the salt-ringed tidemark around the armpits of the animal skin. Nowadays, however, it is no longer a very good idea to thrust your armpit into someone's face in an attempt to impress them. It is a better idea to try and disguise the smell, hence the invention of deodorant, the theory being that if you smell strongly enough of Forest Ferns, no one will ever notice the offensive wafts emanating from your underarm. An alternative, of course, is to leave the sweat for a few months and then grow an actual Forest Fern in your armpit. It might be a bit difficult with fronds sticking out of your shirt but it would be cheaper and might be a bonus in attracting an environmentally-conscious partner.

Deodorants stop you smelling, and should not be confused with antiperspirants, which stop you sweating. The problem with the latter is that you have to sweat from somewhere, so quite often you just end up sweating profusely from whichever part of the body you haven't sprayed. The best thing is to spray your entire body apart from one small circle about 1cm across. All the sweat will then emerge from this one area, and you can use it as a tap. However, make sure you do leave an unsprayed area, or you die like that girl in *Goldfinger* because you have blocked all your pores. Mind you, you do smell very nice. (For the first couple of days.) (H)

Diary, Gary Davies' See over the page.

Dickens, Charles Novelist who tends to give away what his characters are going to do by giving his good characters names like 'Mrs Lovely' and his villains names like 'Mr Complete Bastard'. Thank goodness he didn't design *Cluedo*. 'Er . . . I suspect . . . Mr Murderer . . . In The Kitchen With The Lead Piping. And I think he did it in the kitchen with the lead piping.' (R/D)

MONDAY

15

Woke up with a grapefruit. Can't remember for the life of me where I met it. Put on my boxer shorts - a different one for each day of the week. Always glad when Sunday comes round and I can take all seven off. Usual exercises - said the word 'fun' 50 times and smiled solidly for 35 minutes. Started going to work - then remembered who I was and went to Radio One. Everytime I think of that title 'The Sloppy Bit', it creases me up. Sloppy bit! Hah hah ha! Perhaps time the show ha some new innuendos _ how about plonker willy dicky winky tinkler? (Mu remember to ask someone what all these words mean).

TUESDAY

16

Grapefruit still here. I may have to ask it to leave. Tried to partition my eyebrow. Then realised I'd already done it through major surgery. So tired of being a shallow, trivial person _ bought a copy of The Brothers Karamazov, but it doesn't seem to play at either 33 or 45. Show went well, played Shakata (Palitoys Christmas offering). Hordes of girls waiting for me outside Radio One. They kicked my head in.

WEDNESDAY

17

Dear Diary - No milk today thank you.

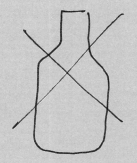

⋄ JUNE ☆⋄★

THURSDAY

18

Got up. A man from Unigate Express Dairy came round with a note that said ' Got up. Grapefruit refuses to go. Bought a pair of industrial tweezers for eyebrow.' Hmm. Seems the milkman lives a very similar life to my own (although apparently a day earlier). A friend for the future? In the evening, was meant to record TOTP, but couldn't get the video to work.

FRIDAY

19

Spent all day getting ready to play the Hippodrome, at Whipsnade Zoo. Then went to a wild party - saw Mandy, Patsy, Sam, kim, Maria et al on their way to a different one. Made double sure not to leave party with any form of fruit - instead came back with a lovely young thing called Barbara.

THE WEEKEND

20

Damn it all - mistook Barbara for 'a banana'. Easy mistake to make.

21

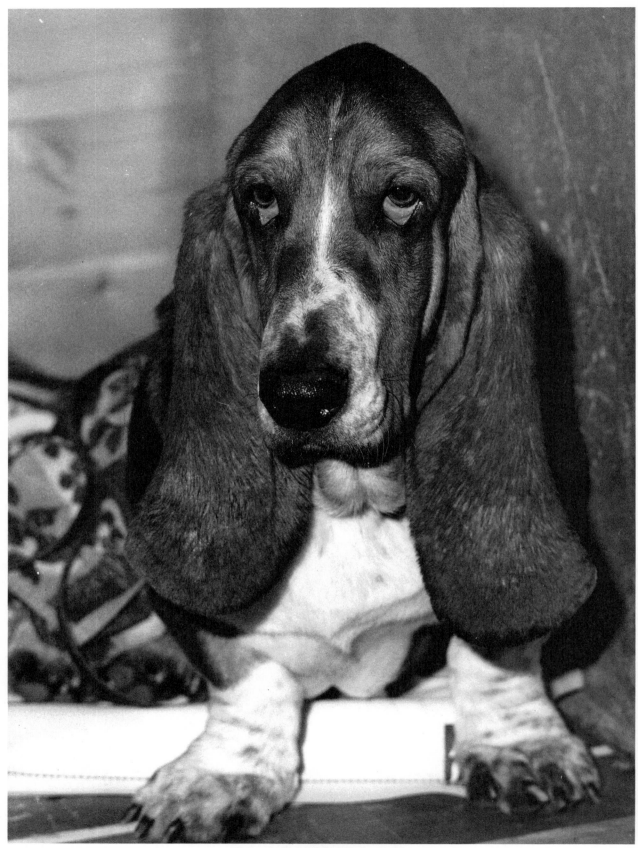

Dogs make happy, boisterous family pets

Dogs There are many types of dogs, including of course the *Great Dane,* of which the most famous is Scooby Doo (*See* DOO, SCOOBY*).* There is also the *St Bernard,* which wanders around the Alps looking for skiers who have been maimed in an avalanche, going up to them and standing there with a barrel of brandy slung tantalisingly around its neck. The injured skier has probably broken both his arms and is therefore totally unable to take advantage of the St Bernard's offering, and the St Bernard knows this; it just stands there, lolling its tongue and taunting the accident victim. Even if the skier has only broken one arm, he still can't get the casket open,

so the St Bernard has the last laugh either way. The only way these dogs could ever be of any use to anybody would be if they could be trained to open the casket themselves with their paws and then pour it into the injured skier's mouth, but then the victim would be drunk when the medical team arrives and instead of allowing them to put him on the stretcher and take him off to hospital, he'd probably pick a fight with them and accuse one of them of fancying his girlfriend.

There is also the *Old English Sheepdog,* which was obviously never any use as a sheepdog since it can't see where it's going. For this reason it

DOGS: The Dulux dog earns £75,000 a year for his TV commercial appearances

was replaced by the collie and given a new job selling paint. One has to hope it doesn't spend too much of its time with its nose dipped in the Non-drip Gloss, or it might be found perched on a second-storey window-ledge claiming it can fly.

Lots of dogs have far worse jobs, like the ones whose job is to smoke cigarettes so scientists can see how fast they get lung cancer. This is obviously completely pointless since dog behaviour bears no resemblance to human behaviour. To have any relevance to human smoking, the dogs would have to sit in restaurants blowing their smoke all over everyone else and moan endlessly about how persecuted they are.

The ones who really have it cushy are *Guide Dogs.* This is because they get to go in all the places where other dogs aren't allowed to go. Shops always have notices that say 'NO DOGS Except Guide Dogs', which means that Guide Dogs are always much more up with High Street trends than other dogs. The Guide Dog will get all the new albums and fashionable clothes first and be able to flaunt them in front of his mates who can't get into the shop. For this reason, Guide Dogs often get mugged, which is why they're always appealing for money to train new ones.

DOGS: Natural vegetarians

ing 'sausages') was Lassie, who was later made into Meaty Chunks.

The most famous book involving dogs is Dodie Smith's *101 Dalmatians,* although the sequel, *303 Squishy Turds on the Pavement,* has never been published.

Dole, The Dole offices have always been designed according to a series of specifications first established in the late 1960s:

> 1. The office must have no carpet. If it does, rip it up and put down some black lino. Then grind into the lino four hundredweight of cigarette butts, and some pre-war chewing gum.

> 2. Do not use air fresheners called things like 'Roseglade' or 'Honeysuckle'. Use ones called 'B.O.'

> 3. A man must be employed to shout and bang on the grille at all times.

> 4. Decorate the office with posters that really rub it in, in particular one that says 'Going on Holiday?'

> 5. Each cubicle must have a meaningless letter above it so that the claimants are never sure if they are in the right queue.

In recent years, the government has been making it more and more difficult to claim the dole. In the 1970s, the form used to say 'Are you unemployed?' to which the answer was 'Yes'. Now it reads more like a medieval witch-trial:

DOLE FORM – B104/Z

"Do you, or any of your dependants, float when thrown into water?"

DOGS; Pit-bull terriers tend to attract a certain type of owner

POODLE; They look stupid no matter how hard you try

Another working dog is the *Police Dog.* There are various sorts of these. Usually they are Alsatians, but some of them spend every working day sniffing for drugs, and after twenty years in the Heathrow customs department, look more like Keith Richards. Others are trained to chase criminals and bite their legs off, but unfortunately, being dogs, they are easy to put off. This was discovered during an armed raid on Walthamstow Nat West in 1986. When one of the raiders threw away his sawn-off shotgun in panic, the dog chased it and brought it back to him. After patting it on the head, he shot it.

Other dogs have to go on *Blue Peter,* like Petra and Shep. Perhaps the most famous media dog (apart from the one that went on *That's Life* say-

But in order to combat the new rigour, we have produced our own booklet to help people fiddle the dole, called *Sign On, Don't Let On.* Here's a short extract:

CHAPTER ONE

THINGS NOT TO DO IF YOU WANT TO CARRY ON GETTING YOUR GIRO

1. Show up at the dole office carrying a ladder and wearing dungarees that say '*Acme Window Cleaning Co.*' on the back.

2. Interrupt your claim interview to make an urgent business call on your vodaphone.

3. When asked 'Have you earned any money in the past two weeks?' say 'It depends on whether Geneva bites on this latest shipment.'

4. Take a job at the dole office.

Donkey Footballer with no skill but who runs about a lot, e.g. Steve McMahon, Denis Wise, Vinny Jones and, quintessentially, Tony Adams. It is part of the English Constitution that there must always be at least four of these players in the national team, although Graham Taylor has recently increased that quotient to eleven. If you are at a football match and one of these players gets the ball, it is customary to shout 'Hee-haw'. (D)

The donkey prides himself not only on how often he boots the ball into touch, but also on how. When the donkey boots the ball into touch, it will always be with a loud thwock of self-righteousness. *Smack.* (R)

Doo, Scooby Large Great Dane belonging to group of amateur ghosthunters – Fred, Daphne, Thelma and the humorously-named 'Shaggy' (on account of his long hair and not, as some authorities claim, on account of his sexual prowess with Daphne). This quartet investigated hauntings in a garishly-decorated van known as the Mystery Machine, which looked like the sort of badly-painted Ford Transit that heavy metal bands buy to drive to gigs in. S.D. was rather

Vinny Jones' soccer skills

Fig. 1. Elbow in face

Fig. 2 Booting the Ball into Touch

Fig. 3 Running around a lot

Fig 4 Late challenge.

cowardly and frequently trembled or ran away – his catchphrases included 'Yikes', 'Raggy!' and 'Oh-Oh – it's a Ghost!' delivered in his inimitable humorous semi-bark. Actually nowadays Fred and Thelma seem to have disappeared to be replaced by the usual Hanna-Barbera girl-with-long-hair-and-large-bust, and Scooby's nephew, Scrappy Doo. Scrappy Doo is the really irritating one who keeps shouting 'Puppy Power!' It's interesting, however, that they chose to make him Scooby's nephew and not his son, because that would have meant the thought of Scooby Doo on heat humping away at some female dog, while Shaggy got a Scooby Snack ready for afterwards.

The existence of Scrappy Doo does mean that Scooby must have a brother or sister, and one wonders what their name is.

Doss A word you don't hear so much anymore. People used to say it a lot, didn't they? 'I'll just doss down at your place', they used to say. 'This place looks like a dosshouse', your mum said sometimes. Now you never hear it. Funny that. (D)

Double Glazing Pro: Keeps your house warm. Con: Makes it look shit.

Down and Out, How To Go . . . Disappear into the cellars and subways, croaking, staked out in the frosted flags of the bus concourse one fine February morning, kidney like a barrel peg and mouth empty of teeth. But where do you begin? Single sheepskin slippers cost and Peruvian-knit tea-cosy hats don't just grow on trees. (R)

Duran Duran Their principal problem was wanting to be a sophisticated adult rock band when all their fans were thirteen. Now that they are a sophisticated adult rock band, they have thirteen fans.

Anwar Sadat

Edgware

Edgware Suburb of London. Originally a small settlement on Watling Street (Roman Road), Edgware now marks the end of the Northern Line on the London Underground. Indeed it was the building of this line in the 1930s that prompted the growth of the suburb.

Even now, however, Edgware's classical heritage is far from forgotten, living on through the building of Corinthian or Doric porches on the otherwise undistinguished semi-detached houses (*See* DIY). The addition of such architectural features usually goes hand in hand with pulling up all the grass in the front garden and replacing it with speckled tarmac, and the purchasing of a mock eighteenth century coach lamp for by the front door. Edgware has quite a large branch of the Abbey National.

Edinburgh, Duke Of, Award Scheme Scheme where awards are given to people who are most like the Duke of Edinburgh. Being Greek, swearing at foreigners and never shagging your wife gets you a gold medal. (D)

Edward VIII King of England who came to the throne in 1936 but abdicated shortly afterwards to marry Mrs Simpson, much to the annoyance of Bart and Homer.

Edwards, Eddie 'The Eagle' A cunt. (D)

Egg Another thing, like cabbage, that it is very bad news to smell of. (D)

Emmenthal Cheese that smells of B.O. (D)

Emu, Rod Hull and *See* EDWARDS, EDDIE 'THE EAGLE'. (D)

Energy With the ever-increasing scarcity of fossil fuels, and the ever-mounting threat of pollution, energy policy is an increasingly vital area of government concern. The best energy-saving advice ever comes from an old school exercise book, which had been bought as part of a job-lot by the BBC Props Dept. The cast of *The Mary Whitehouse Experience* found this gem when rehearsing a sketch about school. The book in question was a physics exercise book and one of the things in it was an exercise in which the pupil had been asked 'Suggest Ten Ways to Save Energy'. In response to this was written:

1. <u>Don't</u> use washing machine – hand wash.
2. Don't eat toast.
3. Learn to play instrument – <u>don't</u> use stereo.
4. Go to bed earlier.
5. Eat more cold food.
6. Buy warm clothes – <u>don't</u> use heater.
7. Watch T.V's in shop windows.

Here, tragically, inspiration ran out. Either that, or the bell went. Who knows what shafts of insight might have constituted numbers 8, 9 and 10? But already, in these seven pearls of reasoning by this anonymous school pupil, we have the basis of an energy conservation policy to put the Government to shame.

The key element of this strategy that marks out the thinker as a true visionary is its meticulous scope. Not only are there broad, sweeping policy areas – *Go to bed earlier* – but there is a keen appreciation of the small details. *Don't eat toast* is a masterstroke. Bread is, after all, already cooked – why on earth should one re-cook it? The reclassifying of toast as a luxury item may cause consternation in some quarters, but in a world with an uncertain supply of fossil fuels, it is a brilliant move. If every British household were to disconnect their toaster, the energy saved could power Birmingham for a week. (Of course, if we were to disconnect Birmingham, we could all eat as much toast as we liked.)

Another mark of genius is the scale of values. Normally, the Department of Energy is unconcerned with the effects of its edicts on the arts, but this thinker has a soul. *Learn to play instrument, don't use stereo.* Why vegetate in front of your rack-system when you can listen to some other member of your family squeak out 'Three Blind Mice' on the descant recorder? (The only opposition to this measure has come from the Samaritans, who say they won't be able to cope.)

Thus far, then, what is envisaged is a nation of stoic, musically-proficient citizens who shun the unnecessary re-browning of bread and have early nights. But what of the community? Surely, what with all the time spent practising one's instrument and doing the hand-washing – not to mention all the time spent spreading butter which, in the bad old toast-days, would have quickly melted – what with all this, there is a danger that the social element of life would be lost. But this danger has been considered, and forms the basis of the last measure – *Watch TVs in shop windows.* One can almost sense the fellowship in the air as a group of citizens, tired after a long day of wringing-out and playing scales, gather in front of Radio Rentals to lip-read *Coronation Street.*

It is obvious to us at *The MWE* that hidden inside an anonymous old exercise book is the work of an undiscovered political seer. The author of these seven measures should be tracked down at once and made Energy Secretary. Advertising agencies will pitch for the privilege of turning *Don't eat toast* into a catchy jingle. The coal industry will howl in protest as demand slumps. Mother's Pride will face bankruptcy. But environmentalists will breathe a sigh of relief that, at last, someone has cut through to the issues that really matter.

Enterprise Allowance Scheme Scheme which, despite what the Government say about it not being there purely to bring down the unemployment figures, and how you can only get on it with a viable business proposition, would still take you if your viable business proposition was the publication of an Arabic version of *The Satanic Verses.* (D)

Espadrilles Shoes that stink even though you've only worn them twice. A word of advice: don't buy them.

Estate Agent The masters of making duff property seem quite nice, so you can waste your time by going round to see it. It would be far more sensible to make the details accurate.

McDONALD

189 Mercers Road
Camden NW39
Tel 0986 897 6785/86
Fax 0986 675 8967

PROPERTY PARTICULARS

14 WEDDERBURN ROAD

We are delighted to offer this unbelievably small and horrid Victorian terraced house. The present owners have lived in the house for 20 years and have systematically removed everything that was original and attractive. Wedderburn Road is an extremely busy and treeless residential road which is used as a cut through to avoid the High Street. All the rooms have double glazing in a vain attempt to reduce the appalling traffic noise

* NO ORIGINAL FEATURES

* NOWHERE TO PARK

* RAILWAY AT REAR

* BRIGHT ORANGE "FLAME DESIGN" NYLON CARPETS THROUGHOUT

* MINISCULE TOWN GARDEN WITH 4 DEAD PLANTS

* RECENTLY RELEASED PSYCHOPATH AT NO 12

The accommodation is arranged on two floors and comprises

ENTRANCE HALL: Terrible smell of gas

RECEPTION ROOM: 9' x 8'. Artex ceiling, spotlighted oil painting of the owner's dog, badly repaired box sash window full of Polyfilla, disgusting black leatherette three-piece suite

BATHROOM: Avocado suite from Texas Homecare, toothpaste-smeared mirror. Furry lavatory suite cover. Rubber shower attachment perished on to taps.
Leak to:-

KITCHEN: 4' x 3'6". Selection of badly fitting cupboards, rubbishy cooker with lots of old peas and breadcrumbs under it. Broken X-Pelair.

BEDROOM 1: Tasteless initialled ceramic fingerplate from holiday in Spain. All white chipboard fitted wardrobes with tacky mock brass fittings

BEDROOM 2: Children's room. A selection of now embarrassing but irremovable pop stickers on wall. Semen stain on carpet.

BEDROOM 3: Too horrid to go in

W.C. 'The smallest room' embossed on door

PRICE: Recently reduced (no one wants to buy it and quite frankly who can blame them

However, this problem has gone on right through history.

Athelfroth and Wulfstan

24 Bubonic Street
Londinium

Estate Agents

Property Details
54 Churl Terrace

As vendor's SOLE AGENTS, we are delighted to offer this exceptional peasant hut in the middle of a sought-after area of swamp. The property has been well looked after by its current owners who have rewattled and daubed extensively. The surrounding area is free of Black Death and the local castle offers safety from pillaging Vikings.

RECEPTION: Mud floor. Open fire. Dead dog acts as draught-excluder.

KITCHEN: Large pot hole in roof. Ample storage for wheat, fowl, etc.

BEDROOM 1: Southern aspect, breezes bring pleasant coolness in summer and help finish off bronchial victims in winter.

BEDROOM 2: Currently occupied by 24 children and another dead dog. Potential to convert to a study.

GARDEN: Quarter of an acre, tithe to local Lord. Grazing for scrawny sheep, etc.

GARAGE: Off-street parking. PRICE; 20,000 groats, 3 sheep or Swap for your Daughter.

E.T. That film by Steven Spielberg, with the alien in it that looks a bit like John Biffen.

Exams There is currently much controversy in education over the exams system, with the Conservatives saying that the political left hold too much sway over the syllabus. According to the Tories, the average examination paper looks like this:

HACKNEY AND HARINGEY EXAMINATIONS BOARD

EUROPEAN HISTORY 1500 – 1900
9-11.30 a.m. Wed. 4 June

Candidates should answer **TWO** questions from Section A and then **AT LEAST ONE** question from each of Sections B and C. Privileged bastards from public schools should answer **FIVE** questions from every section. Marks will be deducted for correct spelling, or being male.

SECTION A

1) 'The British Empire was an evil, repressive regime which terrorised millions of innocent people and ruined their countries.' Discuss. **(Do not take a vote.)**

2) Monarchy is, like, an anachronistic evil. Agree with this statement in not less than 800 words.

3) If you have not understood either of the above questions, then do not worry, because academic achievement is meaningless and is merely used by the establishment to perpetuate class inequalities.

It is a criticism often levelled at exams that they are divisive and elitist, displaying a narrow range of skills and not properly representative of the pupils' full achievements. This is obviously true, and one suggested solution is to introduce special papers specifically aimed at those who, for one reason or another, under-achieve in traditional exams:

LONDON AND COUNTIES EXAMINATIONS SYNDICATE

CRAP AT MATHS A LEVEL
9-12 Noon Tue. 3 June

Candidates should try and have a go at as many questions as they understand. The first couple are fairly easy, and the Plan and Elevation one is a piece of piss. Write on one side of the paper only, if you manage to write anything at all.

SECTION ONE

1) $3x - \{y + 4\} = 24$
What the fuck is all that about? *(2 marks)*

2) Draw an equilateral triangle with 2.5 cm base. Then calculate the apex angle, pretending to use logarithms, but actually using a protractor. Make up some working. *(5 marks)*

3) Draw a circle of 3 cm radius and then **EITHER** a) calculate its radius, **OR** b) colour it in.
(3 marks)

4) Throw a pencil at your mate. *(35 marks)*

Eyes, Stars In Their TV Series presented by Leslie Crowther, which enables men who look nothing like George Michael to come on, go through some dry ice, and come out looking nothing like George Michael. Some may have thought that this apparently innocuous look-alike show could lead to no greater problem than the viewer at home occasionally thinking 'Hang on! Is that really Leslie Crowther? Or could it be an embalmed corpse?

But in actual fact, some disturbing recent events have suggested that the performers on *Stars In Their Eyes* may have darker ambitions than just proclaiming themselves the saddest people in the world

The chilling possibility is emerging that the careers of stars like George Michael could be being usurped by talentless impostors. That this had indeed happened was confirmed by the release of *Listen Without Prejudice* – clearly not the work of a great musical genius but, perhaps, of a fat, unshaven, Greek tosser. In this context, an interview George Michael did a few days after the release of the album is interesting:

'Well, you see, the album that I recorded was actually called *Listen <u>With</u> Prejudice.* It had Gary Bushell and Jimmy Greaves commenting on The Bhundu Boys. The first track was called 'The Bloody Irish Are Always Drunk and Have Got Sideburns'. The second one was a dance number called 'Aretha Franklin Stole My Car Stereo'. The third track was called 'Greeks Are Bent'. Oh, what a giveaway.'

The interview was never printed as it was at this point that the interviewer began to suspect that perhaps this man too may not have really been George Michael. (D/R)

1: Leslie Crowther.

2. A Leslie Crowther look-alike.

3. An embalmed corpse.

George Michael

Fablon The stuff you covered your rough book with, that you could never get the bubbles out of.

Feet An artist's nightmare.

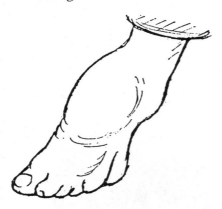

Felching Type of sexual activity. I don't know if I can bring myself to tell you what it means. All right. Steady now. Here goes. Felching is: sucking your own sperm out of a lover's anus. Oh my God, I've got to go and have a bath.

The extraordinary thing about the word 'felching' is, because most people don't know what it means, you could say it on TV more easily than you could say, for example, 'bloody', or 'motherfucking cunt'. It's as if it's on a swearing frequency so high that Mary Whitehouse can't hear

it. Not being a word in common usage, I've recently submitted it to come up on *Call My Bluff*. (D)

Fellatio Type of sexual activity that's never quite as good as men think it's going to be. Oh great, you think, a blow job – and then you can't quite feel anything except the odd tooth. The reality of fellatio, in other words, suffers from a kind of imaginative shortfall. Of course, you say this to a woman and she'll say 'Ah, you just haven't been given a good one', which is a bit like a bloke telling a lesbian she just hasn't met the right man. (D)

Ferodo A company who appear to spend their entire advertising budget having their name painted on urban railway bridges. Not to be confused with

Freddo A masterpiece of marketing by Cadbury's – a chocolate bar moulded into the shape of a slightly elongated frog. Very popular in 1975, but then, so were Showaddywaddy.

Fireflash The aeroplane that looks like Concorde in that episode of *Thunderbirds* where it's on its maiden flight, but the undercarriage doesn't work and it has to land on top of some truck things that Vergil is driving along the runway. Also a word to describe the unusual but factually-recorded phenomenon of spontaneous human combustion whilst indecently exposing oneself.

Fireworks Code, The Real

1. Light the Blue Touch Paper and retire to a safe distance.
2. Watch the firework go 'Sqt.'
3. Think 'Shall I obey the fireworks code?'
4. Think 'Naaah. That rocket cost me two quid!'
5. Go back to the rocket, pour some petrol on it, sit on it, relight it and shout 'Who's going to present *Jim'll Fix It* nowwwwww!!'

Fish In one of his miracles, Jesus did the Feeding of the 5,000; he fed 5,000 people using five loaves and two fishes. It's clear from this that Jesus' gift for oratory was not matched by his grasp of home economics, because obviously, if he wanted just fish and loaves, then he can only have been doing Cod in Breadcrumbs or something, and he would have had far too many breadcrumbs. However, it's unlikely that Jesus would have made a mistake like this, so maybe, if he needed five loaves, then that means that the fish in question were really huge. Come to think of it, if he was feeding 5,000 people, then they probably were. People forget that some fish are really big. So Jesus probably got five loaves, two really huge marlin or deep-sea halibut, and then crumbled the bread into breadcrumbs and served the fish up as goujons.

Also, of course, when considering this miracle, we must remember that out of a random sample of 5,000 people, then probably some of them didn't like fish. Statistically there would have probably been a couple of hundred strict vegetarians who only would have eaten the bread, and if Jesus had used it all up to fry the fish in, then they would have gone hungry. Also, loads of kids hate fish, so out of the 5,000, probably only about 3,000 or so would have actually wanted the food. This is not to denigrate the miracle in any way – I mean, feeding 3,000 people with five loaves and two fishes isn't actually much easier than feeding 5,000. Especially if some of them were greedy.

This shows us how important fish have been in history. When one considers that two-thirds of the earth's surface is sea, and then remembers that the sea is absolutely full of fish, then one suddenly realises that these finny fuckers are really important, and if they weren't so stupid they could have taken over by now. Fortunately, of course, they can't breathe out of water, and this very much counts against them in the world domination stakes. Even the most territorially-ambitious, megalomaniac fish has to face the fact that, for as long as he is reliant on gills, he is more likely to end up in a Bird's Eye Captain's Pie than in any position of real executive power.

Another important thing about fish is that some of them have very silly names. It is very hard to take seriously any creature with a name like *Turbot, Flounder, Dab* or *Guppy*. Other leading types of Comedy Fish are the aforementioned *Halibut;* also *Dogfish, John Dory,* and *Tench.*

Another factor to remember, on the subject of fish, is that *It's the fish John West reject that make John West salmon the best.* This obviously depends on what fish John West reject. If John West is given a load of haddock, then obviously he is going to reject them, on the grounds that they are *not salmon.* This in no way reflects on the quality of the haddock, or indeed says anything about the quality of the chosen salmon. Really, to make any sense, the slogan should have gone *It's the inferior salmon John West reject, that makes John West salmon the best out of the ones John West choose from.*

British and Icelandic fishermen conduct heated negotiations

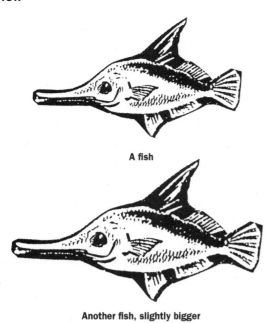

A fish

Another fish, slightly bigger

Fish, More Stuff About Fish are animals that somehow manage to die from eating too much. I mean, it's quite difficult to do that, even when you're eating proper food, y'know, chocolate cake and Spangles and roast duck, but they manage it with little bits of dust. You might imagine that there's a cut-off point where the fish thinks, 'I feel a bit sick now' or 'Perhaps I'll leave that fourth grain for later' but no, it's grain one, grain two, grain three – floating on top of the bowl. (D)

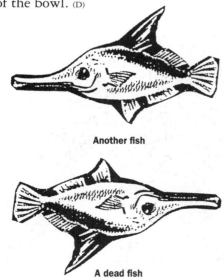

Another fish

A dead fish

Football, Origins of Football matches were first played with a goat's bladder between whole towns called things like Twittingham and Old Sawrey. The pitch would be a whole county and fatalities were not so much expected as applauded.[1] This spectacle can still be seen today whenever three of you go to the park for a kickaround and at first just a couple of lads ask if they can join in. (D/R)

Fractal Geometry Branch of mathematical science which says that certain naturally occurring surfaces form themselves on an internally repeating scale, so that it is impossible, for example, looking at a stretch of coastline, to know whether you are looking at a 1000-mile section or a 1-mile section. In theory, it is equally impossible if you look at a 1-foot section, but there you'd probably see an old tube of Ambre-Solaire and a bit of broken wood with some tar on it, which might give the game away.

French, Andy Friend of David Baddiel's (*See* BADDIEL, DAVID LIONEL) from school, responsible for 'The Andy French Factor', defined as an allowable multiplication to the power of 10 of the amount of girls you've ever got off with. The AFF also allows for an unreasonable exaggeration of the type of sexual activity indulged in.

Example: Haberdasher's Aske's School, Elstree, 3. 2. 77. David Baddiel, aged fourteen, was being interrogated by his classmates as to the facts and figures of his sexual history to date. Up to this point, in actual fact, David had managed one dry kiss with Nadia Peters at a Summer Camp two years previously. However, under the allowances of the Andy French Factor, David was legally entitled to claim this as having got off with ten girls, one of whom he'd actually shagged.

---

[1] With the advent of TV, this style of football eventually died out, as it took commentators well over ninety minutes to read the team line-ups.

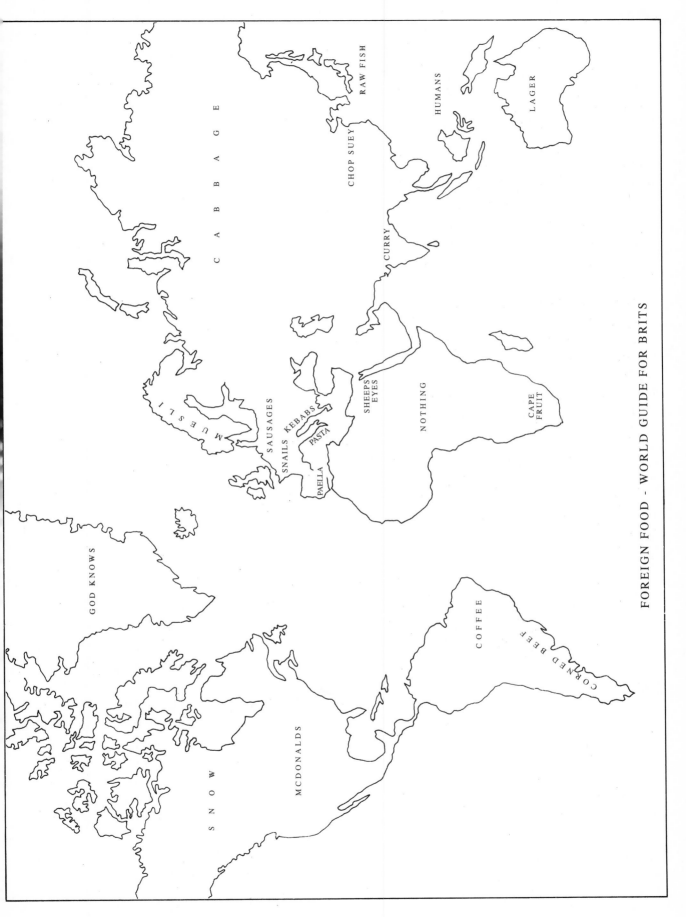

FOREIGN FOOD - WORLD GUIDE FOR BRITS

Simon Lazarus[2] was once successfully prosecuted for misuse of the Andy French Factor, by claiming to have got off with a girl when he hadn't actually got off with anyone ($0^{10} = 0$) (D)

Future, The Present ecologists say 'What sort of future are we leaving for our children?' They don't realise that that is exactly *why* we carry on in the environmentally unfriendly way that we do. Let me explain. When our teenage kids start slagging *us* off, it won't hurt so much because we'll already have got our revenge.

'You're an old fart Dad, a washed-up old stand-up that no one likes.'

'So, you're just off out now then are you son? Well, don't forget your asbestos suit and oxygen mask, will you? Heh heh heh.'

The future we're leaving our children is less an ecological legacy, more a pre-emptive strike. (R)

[2] Then close friend of David Baddiel's, now fucking cunt

G

Gas, Cook-Cook-Cookability, That's the beauty of Really a very good advertising slogan that British Gas should be applauded for sticking with for over 175 years. (D)

Girth One of those words you only hear in pornographic magazines. I mean, if it carried no other resonance apart from 'distance across', you'd hear people say, 'Look at the girth of this lake', or 'Nigel Clough's played that the entire girth of the pitch.' But you don't. You only hear Belinda Box say, 'And it wasn't just the length, it was the girth as well! I knew I was in for a treat as I slipped the waistband of his briefs down, over, across and a couple of yards to the left, etc., etc.' So really the *OED* definition should read: 'distance across (your knob).' (*See also* PENDULOUS) (D)

Goldfinger Should have bought some thicker toilet paper.

Goldfish Catatonically dull pets. Most people only have them because they won them at a fair, where you are conned into doing the hoopla stall by the enticing display of prizes: stolen radios, teddy bears, etc. When you actually do it you end up with a goldfish in a plastic bag. The cheek of it is that you're expected to buy a tank for the bloody thing, even though you didn't want it in the first place. Actually there's no need to do this. The fish is quite happy where it is as long as it gets air, and when it grows bigger you can just transfer it into a carrier bag. Alternatively, if you really don't want it, you can grill it, paint it with silver Humbrol enamel paint, and serve it up as a sardine.

Golf
1. Type of chocolate biscuit.
2. Model of car.
3. Game played by Russ Abbott, Ronnie Corbett, Jimmy Tarbuck and other luminaries of showbiz. Golf's invention is attributed to the Scots, who needed a game which a) didn't require a flat surface, and b) didn't have to be cancelled if deer were wandering about the pitch. One thing to remember about golf is that a golf club is a potentially lethal weapon, and that swinging them around can cause serious injuries. Children should never be allowed to play with golf clubs, and certainly not under the age of about eleven. With the sort of fees they charge at Prince William's school, you'd think they'd have worked that one out.

GOLF; Julius Caesar finds his lost ball (Rome Open, 51 AD)

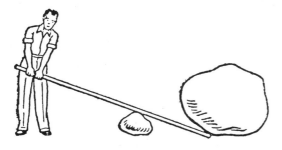

GOLF; It is essential to develop a good swing

Mistake An error, for example putting something in the wrong alphabetical position.

Gothic Architectural style based on the aesthetic habits of the Gothic races. Notre Dame is perhaps the most famous example of Gothic design, but the most classic is undoubtedly the enormous St Francis cathedral in Austerlitz, which is all black, held up with Salon 22 Hard Hold, and has '𝕱𝕴𝕰𝕷𝕯𝕾 𝕺𝕱 𝕿𝕳𝕰 𝕹𝕰𝕻𝕳𝕴𝕷𝕴𝕸' written on the back.

There is only a nominal relationship between Gothic architecture and the Goths, a Teutonic people who in the first century AD appeared to have inhabited the middle part of the basin of the Vistula. Although modern history has imagined the Goths as a fearless, warlike people, this is belied by Plutarch's report of the battle of Macedonia, where he describes them as 'a puny, thin, white bunch in side-buckled pixie boots and bangles who legged it at the first sign of trouble.' Their defeat could, however, have been due in some part to the speech of their Emperor Gordian on the morning of the battle, in which he said, 'Oh, this is a really bad time for me right now – Emma's parents have just split up and Sisters of Mercy have sold out and one of my aunties thought I was a heavy metal fan recently, and well, I started to think about it and we are really – there's not much in it.' (R/D)

Government Information Films Covering such fascinating subjects as smoking in bed, swim-ming when the red flag is flying and the dangers of overtaking on motorways, all these films have one thing in common: they were all made in the 1960s and have never been updated. All the men have Engelbert Humperdinck sideburns and wear tanktops; all policemen ride bicycles; and everybody drives the Austin 1100, which is presumably why overtaking on motorways was so dangerous (*See* CRAP CARS OF THE 1960s). As a result of their age these films have largely lost their impact, to the extent that the natural reaction of anyone watching the film where the bloke falls asleep while smoking and his fag burns his bed, his room and his house to a pile of smouldering ashes, tends to be, 'Well anyone with a haircut like that deserves it quite frankly.'

Anwar Sadat

The effectiveness of these films is also somewhat reduced by the fact that they are only watched by pissed people desperate for something to do after the late film has finished. After eight pints even a film about a chip pan fire can seem like great television and it is for these people that the announcer always says, 'That was a Government Information Film', just in case they thought it was the winner of the Palme D'Or at the Cannes Film Festival.

Possibly the most famous Government Information Film is 'Kerb Drill' *(look right, look left, look right again and if nothing's coming you obviously don't live in London).* In the 1960s this was deemed too simple and was replaced with the Green Cross Code which was immediately to conflict with another Government campaign. One minute you'd be watching a film telling children not to talk to strangers, the next minute two children would be happily chatting away to a large muscular man in green tights, a green shirt, and an old green curtain offering to help them home from school.

Grape Hyacinth Well, once again, the team's a bit stumped on this one, so it's back to the *Britannica:*

> **GRAPE HYACINTH** The name given to any species of *Muscari*, a genus of the lily family (Liliaceae), comprising about 45 species, natives chiefly of the Mediterranean region. They are small, bulbous plants with narrow, fleshy basal leaves and small, usually blue, urn-shaped or globose flowers and . . . *what's that buzzing noise? Oh it's nothing. Anyway,* the common grape hyacinth (*M. botryiodes*), called also grapeflower, baby's-breath and bluebells *no it's definitely a buzzing noise. And I think I can hear my wife moaning as well. Oh well, it's probably nothing.*

Gubba, Tony Football commentator for the BBC who's never quite made it into the Barry Davies/John Motson arena – if the BBC ever get the contract to televise the Zenith Systems Data competition, it'll no doubt be Tony on the lip mike – but who does have a very funny name. (D)

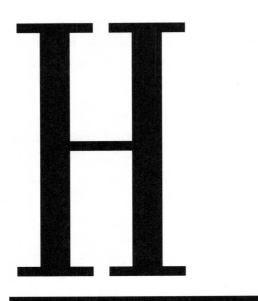

Haddy, Anne Woman who plays Helen in *Neighbours*. A horny bitch, 'I've had Haddy' is a local catchphrase in Melbourne. (D)

Hadrian's Wall A Roman wall which has now fallen down. Serves them right for opting for a plasterboard stud partition on a 2" x 1" frame to save a few bob.

Hawaii Five-0 Cop show in which Jack Lord tried really hard to look twenty years younger

than he actually was, and always said 'Book 'em Danno. Murder one' at the end, thereby showing that murder is so common in the United States it doesn't even warrant a sending off.

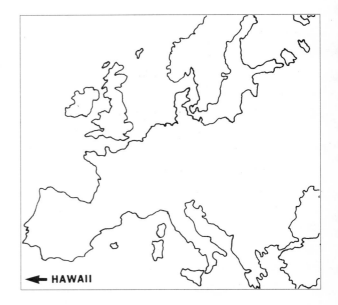

Hawking, Stephen Astro-physicist ten years away from tumbling the secret of black holes until the nervous gods hit him with motor neurone disease. On the cover of *A Brief History of Time* you see, chalked up on the blackboard behind him, hard-core algebra: 'v# (XO # @t+/' and now when he talks, it's like trying to say all that stuff straight out. (R)

Heavy Metal Sub-species of pop music. Usually traced to the British 'blues boom' of the mid-1960s, 'heavy rock' developed via artists like Eric Clapton (Cream), Jimmy Page (Led Zeppelin) and Jeff Beck ('Hi Ho Silver Lining'). Jimmy Hendrix also 'key influence' (i.e. has been massively ripped-off). Form developed through the early 1970s as primarily guitar-based, with leading proponents including Tony Iommi (Black Sabbath) and Ritchie Blackmore (Deep Purple). The latter band produced one of the genre's classics, 'Smoke on the Water',which goes

Duh Duh Duh
Duh Duh Duh-Duh
Duh Duh Duuuuur
Duh-Duh.

Compare this with Black Sabbath's 'Paranoid', which goes

Duh-duh-duh-duh-duh-duh-duh-uh
Duh-duh-duh-duh
DUH DUH DUUUH.

And one can see two distinct forms emerging — fast and slow. For beginners, the following albums are recommended as an introduction to this genre of music:

HEAVY METAL; Fun and fellowship at Castle Donington Festival

VENOMPHALLUS *Devil Bitch on Heat*
Seminal album containing several classic tracks including 'Satan's Harley Davidson (Is Smaller Than Mine)'.

RAVENSPÖO *The Great Brain Robbery*
Concept album. Two months after it was record-ed drummer Magma died after inserting his penis into a Suzuki 850's exhaust pipe. The band's next album, *Scorchnob*, was a poignant tribute.

MASSKILLER *Lucifer in the Sky with Diamonds*
This album became the subject of a court case in the United States. It clearly contains satanic messages, although the case was actually brought on the grounds that the album was 'rubbish'.

Helmet-Head Type of haircut that Andy French (*See* FRENCH, ANDY) used to have. It's a sort of pudding-bowl affair that makes it look like you're wearing a helmet. Pauline Quirke's got one and, coincidentally, she looks a bit like Andy French. (D)

Hippopotamus Silly-looking animal that lives in swamps. Despite its lumbering appearance and ungainly movement, the hippopotamus can perform delicate functions required in microchip-circuitry manufacture. Also the subject of a humorous song by Flanders and Swann, 'Mud, Mud, Glorious Mud'. This latter fact needs to be made clear, since many youngsters nowadays are unfamiliar with Flanders and Swann and think that the song is a tribute to the makers of the immortal Number One hit, 'Tiger Feet'.

HIPPOPOTAMUS; Looks silly

Hoddle, Glenn Brilliant football player who should have had England teams built around him, but of course was left out in the cold because he was too good. Not funny, but I've got it off my chest. (D)

House Plants The thing about house-plants is that they never behave like it says on the little pointed label you find stuck in the pot:

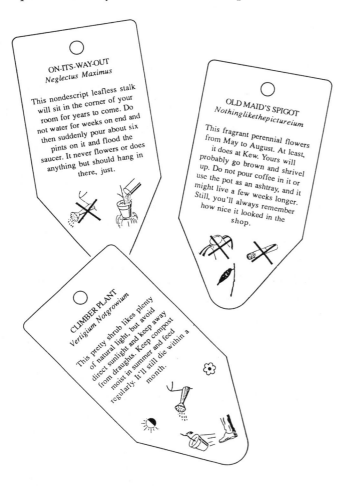

ON-ITS-WAY-OUT
Neglectus Maximus

This nondescript leafless stalk will sit in the corner of your room for years to come. Do not water for weeks on end and then suddenly pour about six pints on it and flood the saucer. It never flowers or does anything but should hang in there, just.

OLD MAID'S SPIGOT
Nothinglikethepictureium

This fragrant perennial flowers from May to August. At least, it does at Kew. Yours will probably go brown and shrivel up. Do not pour coffee in it or use the pot as an ashtray, and it might live a few weeks longer. Still, you'll always remember how nice it looked in the shop.

CLIMBER PLANT
Vertigium Notgrowium

This pretty shrub likes plenty of natural light, but avoid direct sunlight and keep away from draughts. Keep compost moist in summer and feed regularly. It'll still die within a month.

Humperdinck, Engelbert 1960s singer primarily remembered for having a silly name but also for having the biggest recorded sideburns since time began. His albums are still available in the bargain bin at some branches of Woolworths, if you look hard enough underneath all the Jim Reeves compilations. (You can also see a photograph of an Engelbert Humperdinck look-alike in every barber's shop in the country.)

Hysterectomy My mother's went all wrong, and for ten years my dad was putting his dick in her ear – before they sent him to prison. (R/D)

I

Igloo House that eskimos live in. It's always seemed a bit stupid to me. I mean, it's cold at the North Pole, isn't it? There's a lot of snow about. So it might seem sensible to build houses you can put central heating into. Instead they sit about in a tent made of ice and wonder why they have to wear furry anoraks indoors. The attempts of many eskimos to put central heating into their igloos have been frustrated by the fact that they wake up the next morning with four radiators and no house. (D)

Following recent events, the Indian Cabinet decides to employ a flower tester.

'Impulse' Advert Advertising campaign whose slogan is expected to change in the light of Rajiv Gandhi's assassination: 'If someone you don't know suddenly offers you flowers – run like fuck!'

Inches, Twelve Size of David Baddiel's penis (*See* PENIS, DAVID BADDIEL HAS A VERY BIG).

Income, Rob Newman's A ridiculously large sum. There is a saying in business circles: 'I've done a Newman', meaning I've earned over £300,000 in a week. Recently, the Ethiopian Government asked our Government not to provide any more aid through GNP percentages or charity appeals, but simply to ask Rob if he could spare a bit of change. He has recently come in as a new buyer for Paul Gascoigne. (D)

Inn What they always call pubs in crap Hammer horror movies, because they think it sounds more frightening.

Insomnia Disease suffered from by David Baddiel (*See* BADDIEL, DAVID LIONEL). A crap disease to have, because no one really thinks of it as the major problem it is: insomnia involves all-night domination by a five-second tape loop of whatever is No. 17 in the charts. And you have to put up with other people telling you they always fall asleep as soon as they get into bed; you know the sort of people: Henry Kelly's wife, Derek Jameson's wife, Prince Charles. (R/D)

Intravenous Way of feeding people through a tube. Sometimes the tube is put up their noses, which, considering that a lot of old people are fed this way, may explain the smell that comes out of their noses (*See* CABBAGEY). (D)

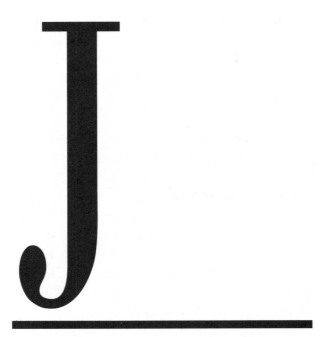

Jelly Tastes horrid but wobbles in a sort of comedy way making it popular at children's parties, but there again so are children's entertainers and they are *crap*.

JESTER; His job was to look like a prat

Jester A jester was a medieval comedian. Lots of people don't realise that jokes have existed since the dawn of time. The ancient world possessed many famous comedians, such as Ramara of Sumeria (d. 789 BC) whose most famous joke was 'What's the fastest animal on earth? – a Mesopotamian with a luncheon voucher', which was very funny to anyone living between the Tigris and Euphrates in the seventh century BC. Amongst the famous Roman jokes we find 'How many citizens of Pompeii can you fit in the back of a chariot? – all of them, if you've got a shovel.'

Jesus Jones Only went to see them 'cos I thought Mike Edwards was Darlene off of *Roseanne.* Not great live performers, unlike Stevie Wonder pictured opposite. (R)

Jewish Noises Here is table of Jewish noises. (R)

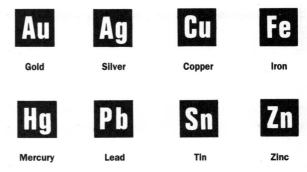

Au	Ag	Cu	Fe
Gold	Silver	Copper	Iron
Hg	Pb	Sn	Zn
Mercury	Lead	Tin	Zinc

Job Ads These, of course, have to be read very much between the lines:

'Hello Dallas!!'

K The letter that students always use to replace 'c' in rag mags and things because they think that it is kool not to be able to spel proply, which in fact is just wanc, illiterate and reinforcing the stereotype of all students as prats. Almost as popular as a rag mag technique as mock (sorry, mok) graffiti.

Kant, Immanuel Smartarse German cousin of Brian Cant (*See* CANT, BRIAN).

Keegan, Kevin The player you always had six of in soccer stars and were desperate to swap for someone more obscure like Dick Kryzwicki (who used to play for West Bromwich Albion or something).

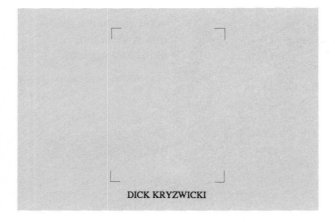

DICK KRYZWICKI

Kentucky Fried Chicken Much copied fast-food outlet, e.g. Tennessee Fried Chicken, Maryland Fried Chicken and the slightly sadder Kennington Fried Chicken.

Kettle Thing you boil water in if you want to make a cup of tea, or kill ants (*See* BOILED ANT). The strangest thing about kettles is the expression 'That's a whole different kettle of fish'. Why would anyone want to put fish in a kettle? Surely this would make your tea taste horrible. And if you've got a kettle of fish, why would you want another one?

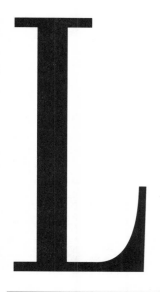

Ladies, Old Impossible to imagine that these people have got vaginas somewhere. (R)

Lecter, Dr Hannibal Psychiatrist, perhaps most famous in this country for his problem page in *Woman's Realm*.

Lederhosen Comedy German leather shorts. Most people assume that the image of the Germans as a nation of lederhosen wearers is a clichéd and xenophobic creation of the British. This is not the case. They wear them almost all the time, and therefore deserve to be ridiculed.

Leeds Utd Glory team of the early 1970s spearheaded by Billy Bremner and Allan 'Sniffer' Clarke, who won both League and Cup by kicking the shit out of their opponents. Also introduced the short-lived custom of wearing little numbered tassles on their sock tie-ups and doing a simultaneous, eleven-man, 360-degree

Dear Doctor

DR LECTER ANSWERS YOUR LETTERS

**Dear Dr,
I recently discovered that my teenage daughter has been taking money from my purse. Should I confront her about it, or is it just a phase she will grow out of ?
Yours sincerely,
Eileen, Essex**

Dr Lecter writes: Did you sodomise her? Did you, Eileen? Perhaps when pubescent she could only get pocket money from you through the performing of expert cunnilingus on Auntie Dora. Because you are, are you not, the very Eileen who in 1967 escaped police detection but not mine after a pin-down/pornography scandal in the Billericay area. Purse-vagina, vagina-purse. Eileen Essex = Ex-Nielsen, does it not? With just an S and an E left over, I think. Ah, how you give yourself away. (Oh, also you haven't got the second N.)

• • • • • • • • • • • • • •

**Dear Dr,
I've noticed that there is a bit of damp** forming on my kitchen wall, and I'm worried that this might give my three-year-old son a bit of a chill,
**Yours,
Norma, Manchester**

Dr Lecter writes: Why? Why does that worry you, Norma? What is there to fear in the sight of goosebumps forming on the taut and tender pale flesh? Petrified that it might attract you, as it attracted Uncle Frank to you that freezing February night in the ranch barn in. . .

Manchester. The wheel has come full circle and I have a lapful of sperm.

• • • • • • • • • • • • • •
**Dear Dr,
I have recently begun killing women because I want to build a suit out of woman's skin. Any advice?**

£5 Star Letter of the Week

Dr Lecter writes: Two shoe boxes make an excellent pair of breasts if you're a couple of victims short.
• • • • • • • • • • • • • •

'Oh Ethel – time I got a new colostomy bag. This time without any ships in it.'

wave to the crowd before kick off. In the second division for most of the 1980s, ha ha. (H)

At all other football grounds including Chelsea, NF fanzine *The Flag* sells about six copies. At Leeds, however, *Flag* sale-returns are used to give attendance figures. (As, in fact, they are at Chelsea.) Leeds fans are of lower intelligence: the only reason they don't throw bananas at black players is because they're worried it's an incentive. (R)

Leopold I Absolutely no idea. (R)

Lepidoptery Escapes me just at present. I'll come back to it. (R)

Library Building in which it is impossible to be for more than thirty seconds without getting the horn. The aphrodisiac power of the library is such that, once inside, even Bernard Levin would find his prim, 1920-ration-book-London-Brighton genitals stirring across and up the left-hand side of his grey worsted pants for the first time since the publication of *The St Petersburg Years*. Alternatively, were Teddy Prendergrass to enter a library he would spontaneously combust.

There are two schools of thought as to why this should be so. The first, based on how anti-sexual a library is obviously *meant* to be, maintains that the libido sets up a deliberate antagonism in response to this bold attempt of the superego to put it on ice for a while. It senses a conscious attempt to banish it from the action and, like a spoilt child in the hands of an unauthoritative parent, responds by showing off even more loudly than usual.

Anwar Sadat

The second, more radical, school of thought insists that libraries are actually sexual, through a tragic catalogue of design flaws. First, the 'quiet please' sign. They might as well put up a sign saying 'tense sexual atmosphere please', or 'Furrowed guilt in the air at *all times*', or 'No standing on the desk and shouting "Hey, everybody – let's fuck!!" like you desperately want to.' Second, the presence of magazines covered in plastic leading to a confusing similarity with a sex shop. Third, the presence of far too many fifteen year olds reading books.[1] (R/D)

Lighting Up Times The bit at the back of the

---

[1] The one library in the world which does not conform to this rule is the Willesden Green Community Library (bus routes 8, 16a). We can't quite work out why this is. It's something to do with scuffed parquet flooring, the seemingly endless big-print section, the notices on the pinboard like 'Going to a Post Office: A Retard's Guide', the fact that everyone in there has appeared in a BBC2 documentary about the suffering caused by NHS waiting-lists. All this, coupled with the overwhelming presence of tramps pretending to read *Der Spiegel* upside down.

paper, just under the weather forecast, that tells you when the street lights come on in different parts of the British Isles. Read by people who are interested in when street lights come on in different parts of the British Isles.

Loonies Mental people.

HISTORY

In past centuries a loony would have a difficult time getting recognition, as all the things that mark them out today – talking about Kaiser Wilhelm I, crapping out of the window, wearing out of date clothes and saying that you're an ostler by trade – were all thought of as normal. I mean, if crapping out of the window isn't going to get you put into Shenley, what is?

NAPOLEON COMPLEX

The Napoleon Complex is the name for the mental disorder in which the patient is convinced that he or she is Napoleon. This is one of the classic psychological disorders, and goes right back to the early nineteenth century, when the French psychologist Dr Jean Jacques-Papin appears to have been faced with one of the rare incurable cases, or, as he terms it, 'un rejecte de Shenley'.

Jan 3, 1799. Saw Patient N again today. The problem appears to be worsening. He claims to have taken control of the 'revolutionary government' and has established himself as Emperor. Noticed that he has begun placing his left hand inside his right jacket breast. This is all typical.

Aug 14, 1810. Patient N approaching crisis stage. He seems to be going to such extremes to convince me, that he has even raised an army of 10,000 cavalry and 50,000 infantry and

invaded Prussia. Suggested he writes a list of ten things he likes about himself.

Sept 15, 1812. Saw N today - v. depressed, but still, alas, wearing three-cornered hat. Claims to have suffered 'heavy losses' at Sebastopol. Tried to cheer him up by playing that new overture by Tchaikovsky with the cannons.

Jean Jacques-Papin's attempts to treat this particular case of Napoleon complex failed to such an extent that eventually Patient N had him executed by the Garde Elite on the palace steps at Versailles.

CLOTHES

Under the Care in the Community scheme, a cramped Sherpa van drives all modern loonies from Shenley to a South Molton Street outfitters. Here they're fitted for purple high-heels three sizes too big, a weasel stole and a toy handbag. 'Perhaps sir would like to try on these knackered white headphones off a 1970s hi-fi?' And kitted out with the plastic bags and bobble hats, £35 and the address of a Bed & Breakfast.

Lute Medieval musical instrument popularised by Sir Prancelot.

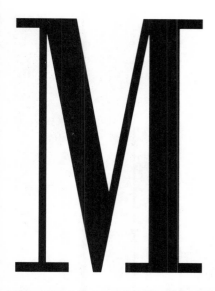

Magellan (*See* DENNIS, HUGH)

Marx, Karl Marx was an old man with a big grey beard who spent all day in the library. In fact, the reason he took six years to complete *Das Kapital* was not actually, as Engels claimed, because he could not solve the contradiction between surplus value and superstructure, but because he was always being thrown out for being a tramp. A long-standing argument with the British Library took the form of Marx claiming that it was going to take fourteen volumes to truly analyse the structure of capitalism, against the head librarian's claim that he was just in there because of the wet weather.

In fact, there may be more in the British Library's view of Karl Marx than modern scholarship allows. If you read *Das Kapital* (or at least the three pages you can get through without feeling a little drowsy and in need of an orgasm) what is it? A series of obsessive and rambling monologues on the subject of money, such that at any moment you expect him to start going on about how he killed a copper in Stevenage once and the pipes are calling, Oh Danny Boy! the pipes, the pipes . . . (*See* MACLAFFERTY, MAD JACK). (R/D)

Masons Freemasonry is a grand, solemn and mysterious tradition, whose most famous members are Fred Flintstone and Barney Rubble. One of the closely guarded secrets in masonic history is how Fred and Barney managed to perform the all-important masonic initiation ceremony of rolling up the left trouser-leg when they only ever wore leopard-skin leotards. Mr Flintstone was eventually dismissed from The Grand Order of Water Buffalo for using a brontosaurus as a crane, and ordering some pork ribs so big his car toppled over.

The first official records of freemasonry date from 1542, a time when there was no police, no judiciary and no BBC, and therefore no freemasons. However, a close look at these official records does reveal this phrase: *Oh Lulu, how can I get to look like you?* Apparently, the early recorders mistook Freemasons for Freemans, and this may explain why, to this very day, all masons wear front-pocketed trousers and grey windcheaters.

Freemasons were originally groups of builders, and this still plays a large part in its rituals today – the initiation ceremony at The Grand Order of Boaz in Pinner, for example, requires all new members to read a copy of the *Star* and then put on a pair of trousers specially designed to reveal at least five inches of buttock cleft. They then have to repeat the famous 'swearing-in' oath, '*In vestito pendo magnum hymnatia verum depende*', which, literally translated, means 'Oo put those joists there? 'Ckin cowboys. It's gonna cost yer.'

The belief that masons are able to get away with murder was borne out by the career of Jack the Ripper. It is now firmly established that all the Ripper's victims were killed in strict accordance with masonic ritual. The possibility exists, therefore, that famous contemporary detectives were deliberately ignoring clues as to the identity of the murderer in order to shield a fellow mason. This possibility may form the sub-text of a strange unpublished short story by Sir Arthur Conan Doyle:

We arrived at the scene of the girl's murder. It was an ugly sight. I asked Holmes what he made of it.

'Well, Watson,' he said, ' Let's take a look at the evidence.'

'Well,' I replied, 'We've got the knife . . .'

'Yes.'

'And here's what looks to be a shred of his cloak,'

'Hmmm . . .'

'And here's his wallet, his kidney donor card, some passport photos, a collection of person-alised name tags, his diary, including under-neath today's date the sentence "Kill a prosti-tute?", and lastly some headed notepaper on which is written the word "Nipper", crossed out, then "Dipper", crossed out, and finally "Ripper", with a large tick next to it.'

'Frankly, Watson,' said Holmes after a moment's consideration, 'I'm baffled. Fancy a shag?'

(Sir Arthur Conan Doyle, *Holmes Has an Off-Day For Some Reason*, MS: British Library, 213–14).

Then there are other perversions of justice. In 1954, for example, Capt. P.G. Stratford was charged with drunk-driving his car through the local primary school, killing all of the Junior Mixed Infants, and then tossing a grenade into Hattie Jacques' cleavage. Further investigations revealed that Capt. Stratford had also been run-ning a secret concentration camp in St Albans. After pleading guilty, Justice Arthur Picklewickle cautioned Capt. Stratford for hav-ing the same initials as a make of tea. It later came to light that the Captain was a mason. Justice Arthur Picklewickle, however, was not a mason: he was simply a mad cretin.

Ronald Shufflebottom

Another man who fell foul of misinterpreting masonic allegiance in court was Ronald Shufflebottom, who attempted to get himself off a charge of indecently assaulting a sash window by hitting himself on the head and touching his right ankle with his left hand, only to find him-self given an extra six months for doing a Bavarian slap-dance in court.

Lastly, how do you spot a mason? There are certain essential basic attributes: a brown Crimplene suit, a semi-detached house on the A1 and, most importantly, vinegary B.O. There is no doubt, however, that masons have become adept at blending in with the crowd, and per-haps the only thing which just occasionally gives them away is a tendency to wear huge buf-falo heads. So if you see anyone with an enormous buffalo head, it means one of two things: either it's a mason, or it's a buffalo. One way to sort out this confusion is to interview him for a job as Chief Constable of the West Midlands Police Force, at which point he will either a) raise his right hand to his left temple, or b) crap all over the floor and then migrate in a majestic horde to the prairies of Canada. (R/D)

Menus One of the most irritating things in the world is the excessively jokey menu. Especially when it has a 'concept'. (see over page)

Military Insignia The ranks of the British Army.

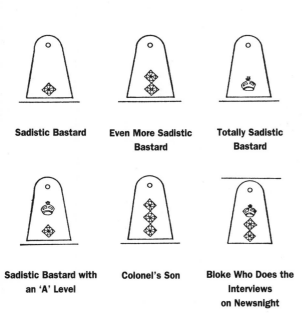

| Sadistic Bastard | Even More Sadistic Bastard | Totally Sadistic Bastard |

| Sadistic Bastard with an 'A' Level | Colonel's Son | Bloke Who Does the Interviews on Newsnight |

| Very Senior | Very Very Senior | Man with Moustache and Red Nose |

Old Enough to Remember First World War   **Completely Senile**

Mission Impossible American cop/secret service show starring Peter Graves (the white-haired bloke who looks a bit like Leslie Nielsen) in which the closed circuit camera systems, heat-sensitive body alarms and highly trained security guards at top secret government research establishments are powerless against the cunning ploy of someone walking up to the front gate in an overall, carrying a tool box and claiming that he has come to fix the air conditioning.

Model T-Ford Early car with a top speed of 25 mph, but which still, as far as can be deduced from all archive film, managed to take all corners at 70. (R/D)

Morris Dancing
1. A strange ritual dance performed by owners of Morris Marinas, which took place by the side of busy main roads. The Marina would sit spewing steam and green water over the tarmac while the owner danced round it, hitting it with a stick and chanting the traditional words: 'I'm never buying another British car as long as I bloody live.'
2. The most embarrassing of all English folk traditions. It survives only to provide an item on the regional news on the first day of summer.

Morris Ital Leyland thought that if they gave it a bigger boot, and called it the Ital (from Italy, geddit?), no one would notice that this was a Morris Marina. It didn't work.

Morrison, Jim He is remembered most for his line 'No one here gets out alive'. A bathroom safety-hazard alert. (R)

Mountain Bike Basically a 16-geared, wide wheeled Raleigh Wayfarer without the saddle-bag, mudguards and bell. Originally designed to cope with the mountainous, rugged and rocky terrain of the Appalachians, it is now very

FLATLINERS

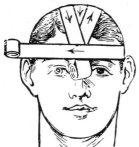

PRE-MED

Calm those nerves. Don't get needled

BARIUM MEAL
Hand-reared chicken, lightly panfried and served with a radioactive isotope. £1.95

NIL BY MOUTH
Ideal if you're thinking of having major surgery! So horrid you won't want to eat again for 24 hours. Boiled potatoes, boiled cabbage, cold lamb and a stewed tomato. £2.15

STOMACH PUMP
A delicious mixture of spiced pork, poppadoms, ice cream, toast, braised liver, peanuts, crisps and lager all topped off with vodka and a selection of Porky scratching! £2.25

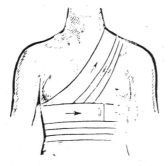

DIALYSIS
Kidneys and liver in a white wine sauce. Don't try it . . . it's offal!

THE OPERATION
. . . Get them under the knife.

STRAIGHT FROM THE HEART
Aortic clots, ventricle and pulminory artery in a warm Hollandaise sauce. Only joking! It's sausages... which is probably the same thing. £5.50

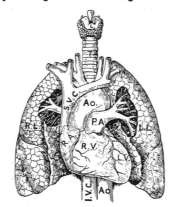

EGG-TOMY
. . . Eggs benedict. Let's hope you've got the balls to try it. £6.25

LOBO-TOMY
Lobster brain with tomato. £6.50

ITLOOKSLIKEEGGTOMY
. . . Absolutely right, only this time it's fried, ha ha. £7.25

PENNE-CILLIN
. . . Pasta shells with mushroom £6.50

DEAD ON ARRIVAL
. . . Well all except the bacteria that is! An inch thick slab of prime beef we bought a fortnight ago and forgot to put in the refrigerator. £7.15

X-RAY
That's exactly what it is! A dead flat fish. £6.90

GANGREEN
Chef's salad. A selection of seasonal vegetables topped with crispy bacon and slivers of condemned camembert. £5.95

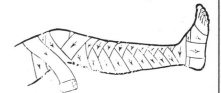

COMING ROUND
. . . These will really wake you up!

DEATH BY CHOCOLATE
. . . A slab of chocolate and fresh arsenic. £1.95

STRETCHER CASE
. . . Eat this and you'll be one . . . double double chocolate mousse with horseradish sauce. Yum Yum. £2.70

FLATLINER SPECIAL
We're flatliners but your stomach won't be. Rich indigestible rum truffle. £2.50

INTENSIVE CARE
. . . Not something we've taken! Fruit salad from a tin. £2.95

Coffee and tea are both very bad for you . . . only joking . . .but they are £3.50 a cup. We're doing it for your own good!

MOVIES
RESTAURANT AND BAR

OPENING CREDITS

AVOCADO BOGART
Guess Bogey woulda approved of this one. Hey, avocado even looks like a bogey. **£1.95**

JAWS
A salad with some tuna in it. Well, it's a fish, and so is a shark. All right, it isn't. **£2.15**

PORKY'S REVENGE
Crap film. And this starter's just as crap; just a few old bits of bacon and some lettuce.And in our version you don't even get any flashes of tit and bum. **£1.95**

- - - - - - - - -

THE MAIN FEATURES
Fresh from the Grilling Fields

STEAK-OUT
8 oz of prime cow flame-broiled just the way Richard Dreyfus and Emilio Estevez would like it. Oh, you haven't seen the film. **£5.50**

THE SILENCE OF THE LAMBS
And why are they silent? Because we've slaughtered them and made them into chops, that's why. With Foster Sauce. **£6.25**

THE GRAD-U-ATE
A plump breast of chicken in a Cajun sauce. Er. . . well, Dustin Hoffman's probably eaten chicken. **£6.65**

FRENCH CONNECTION
A huge pile of garlic, snails and stuff with some heroin in it. Watch out, Gene Hackman's lookin, for ya! **£7.00**

WE ARE SWEDISH NYMPHOS
Ho ho ho! **£6.65**

- - - - - - - - -

CLOSING CREDITS
The Unbearable Lightness of Pudding

CLAPPERBOARD LOADER
Chocolate pudding actually. **£1.75**

ASSISTANT DIRECTOR
Bog Standard Pie, but we have to relate it to films see? **£1.90**

KEY GRIP
Ice cream, with some keys in it. Watch out for your teeth! **£1.50**

- - - - - - - - -

SUPPORTING FEATURES
Couldn't think of a joke!!

SIDE SADDLE
Sounds a bit like `side salad'

E.T.
Egg and tomato salad

TERMINATOR
Strychnine in a bun

CARRY ON SCREAMING
You will when you see the bill

popular in the towns and cities of south-east England as it is by far the most expensive and posey bike you can buy.

Mouth Organ A device for collecting saliva now erroneously thought of as a musical instrument. (D)

Musical Instruments

GRAND PIANO; You need a posh house for this bastard

BAGPIPES; The Scots seem to like it

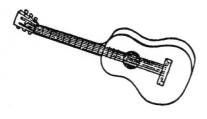

GUITAR; This is an acoustic one like the Gypsy Kings use. Also heavy metal bands use them on their token ballad

FRENCH HORN; Sounds a bit rude

TUBA; Tubby was one

ACCORDION; Rolf Harris used to sometimes play one of these until he discovered something even more crap - the Stylophone

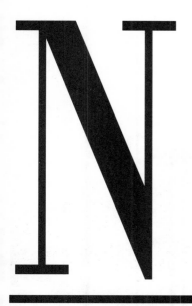

Name, Middle The name you try and hide because it is so crap. Often it is a name that has been passed from generation to generation through the family and which you have been given to keep your granny happy. This knowledge is sod all use when you are having the shit beaten out of you in the playground for being called Windermere.

Names, Poofy Nigel, Clarence, Clement, Maurice, The 8th Marquess of Queensberry, Harley Fleur-Ponce Ponce-Lavender, anything French, and Jane. (D)

Nature Trek The shoes Hugh wore to school. The unique Polyveldt sole made these shoes the footwear equivalent of radioactive waste: incredibly long-lasting and virtually impossible to dispose of. As they also looked completely disgusting they were a nightmare for the child who had been bought a pair and whose mother wasn't about to buy him any different ones until they had worn out. In this case desperate measures were called for. Generally the shoes proved unaffected by both melting in the oven, or accidental acid spillages in the Science lab. However, satisfaction could be found in the use of a large-bore masonry bit and a high-speed Black and Decker hammer drill.

Newman, Robert By day – just a sad and lonely bastard, and by night – asleep.

Personal motto: No Smash Hits, no comment. Some nights, though, I think 'No, I won't be a bedsit ghost.' I fling open my wardrobe double-doors, take out my hippest garments, array them on the bed, and climb into the wardrobe and shut the doors.

Heroes: John Davidson (Tourette's Syndrome Kid), Julie Burchill.

R.D. Laing believed you can trace character back to conception – that the person you are could be conditioned by the fuck that made you. My parents were both teenagers, it was just an urgent sex-thing, a dumb, stupid, pointless fuck – and, lo and behold, so am I. (Laing's theory also accounts for a life spent worrying if I've locked the door.)

Hymns: 'To Be A Pilgrim', 'Dear Lord and Father of Mankind'.

Born: 7/7/64 (After six weeks in the Salvation Army Mothers' and Babies' Home, Hackney, I finally selected some suitable parents and moved to the countryside.)

I grew up among Italians, and as a kid there was this one shop I used to hate having to walk past. Whenever I did the shopkeeper would come out on to the stoop and go 'Hey you! I fuck ya mother! I fuck ya mother!' And I'd shout back 'Hello Dad'.

Some questions and answers:
Q. Is there any subject you wouldn't make a joke about?
A. Gloria Estefan having a two-foot steel girder up her arse.

The Newman family realise they have come out dressed for the wrong decade

Q. What do you do when you can't sleep?
A. Toss and turn in my bed for long hours, racked by guilt, doubt and self-loathing.
Q. Bow, hand and rotary are all types of what?
A. Drill.

When I retire I shall read books on human psychology by way of looking up the answers after a baffling test. Either that, or I shall be in immense pain and have to be helped to the toilet every half-hour.

Nicaragua Country that was for a long time the cause célèbre of the British right-on classes and then the British right-on classes were well sussed. The collapse of the Sandinista regime allowed for certain opinions to be expressed openly which previously could only be held in private.

First, Nicaraguan coffee tastes like shit. No wonder they had to export it all to Camden market. Certain brands of Brazilian coffee may be made through the sweat of exploited workers, but Nicaraguan coffee is made *out of* the sweat of exploited workers.

Second, Latin music is shit. And all you students who thought that the lyrics were all about revolutionary socialism are sussed again, because all they ever actually were were reworkings of 'Ay Yi Yi Yi Moosey'. (R/D)

Nielsen, Dennis Serial killer who escaped detection despite plumbers finding human remains in his drains. The plumbers decided that what was needed was a new washer. In fact he was only rumbled after sending a letter to *That's Life.* (R)

Nietzsche, Friedrich German soccer star who, after a bright start at SV Hamburg, played over 350 games for Frankfurt and captained the national side in the 1890 World Cup. After retiring with a knee injury he wrote a number of books including *The Tactics of the Indirect Free-Kick, The Off-side Trap,* and *The Birth of Tragedy from the Spirit of Music,* which led to a new career in philosophy. Scored hits with *The Genealogy of Morals* and *Also Sprach Zarathustra.* Amongst his ideas were that some races were superior to others and that Jews were an inferior and evil influence. Basically, let's face it, he was just Hitler with an A level.

Numismatics Well, none of us even knows what this is, so it's definitely time to refer back to the *Britannica* :

> **NUMISMATICS (from the latin *Numisma,* a coin) is the study of coins and medals. Coins were first issued in the east and west in the eighth century BC.** *Oh God, there goes the bloody doorbell. Hang on. . . .*
> *Sorry, I've just had to let a workman in. Don't know what he's come for. Anyway,* **the principal mixtures in which coins are struck are electrum, gold, silver, copper and bronze. Electrum is a natural mixture of gold and silver which was used for the earliest Greek coins struck in Asia Minor (Lydia)** – *Oh that's good, he's fixed the buzzing noise.* **Electrum was the metal of the great fifth-century coinage of Czyicus.** *I must say, my wife seems very pleased about it. She's shouting with joy. What's she saying? 'Fuck me! Fuck me! Fuck me!' Well, I can't blame her; I must say, I'm always surprised when workmen fix things these days as well!*

Dear Esther,
I thought you and the That's Life team would like to know that I have a dog which can say 'murder some more rent boys Dennis, go on, chop them up, cook them and put them down the drain.'

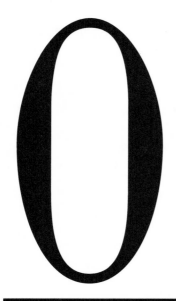

zoos, of course, don't have any sand to bury their head in, so if you want to annoy the zoo-keeper, go up to the ostrich cage and shout loudly at the ostriches. This really frightens them, and they try and bury their heads in the sand. But since the floor of the cage is made of concrete, they usually end up concussed.

Anwar Sadat

Oligarchy A society ruled by oligs.

Olympics, The The Greeks invented sport, and with it the Olympic Games, named of course after the Greek national airline: proof that their inflight service was legendary even then. The first Olympics was staged at Olympia, a large exhibition centre in Athens which also staged the Greek Ideal Home Exhibition, until Plato proved that there was no such thing as an Ideal Home.

Origami An interesting hobby, if you like folding pieces of paper.

Ostrich Large flightless bird (*See* FLIGHTLESS BIRDS). Not only can the ostrich not fly, which really makes you wonder why it bothers being a bird at all, but also when it's frightened, it *buries its head in sand*. What a crap mammal. I mean, what could possibly be more frightening than having your head buried in sand? You wouldn't be able to breathe, or see. And suppose the surface on which the ostrich was standing *wasn't sand*. It'd have to go away, hire a pneumatic drill, and dig down until it found something soft enough to bury its head in. Ostriches in

Ottoman Empire The Roman Empire bequeathed history, law, sanitation and roads; the Greek Empire literature, philosophy and civic responsibility. The Ottoman Empire, while similarly conquering most of the known world, did it all in the name of the Ottoman – a type of pouffe-cum-sofa without a back or arms. The Ottoman conquest can be dated from 1291 when Osman I addressed a gathering in Constantinople saying 'I would like to see a type of pouffe-cum-sofa without back or arms in every home in Macedonia, Mesopotamia and the Visigoth regions of the north.' The crowd responded: 'What – do you mean an Ottoman?' To which Osman I replied: '*Ottoman.* That's the word, of course. Sorry.'

Twenty years later, 30 million men and women lay slain and 200 countries destroyed, but Osman I had achieved his aim. Those who did not conform to his regime were classed as heretics and punished severely: in 1302, following his refusal to give up his chaise-longue, Saint Augustine was burnt at the Ottoman.[1] Despite such cruelty, the Ottoman Empire did create a new source of culture. Drama abounded, particularly in the work of Ummahl, now considered the Sophocles of the East. His greatest tragedy is *Constantine*, in which a man loses an Ottoman, and his greatest comedy, *Hooray!* in which a man owns two Ottomii.

The Empire continued at strength until 1343, when, following the defeat of the Athenians, Osman I held a victory supper in his battle-tent. After the hearty meal, he stretched out his legs, put his arms up and fell over backwards, spilling wine all over his white tunic. Unable to reconcile himself to the fact that this might imply a fundamental design fault in the Ottoman, and that to remedy it would involve the whole thing basically becoming an armchair, he threw himself on to his sword. The next day, his generals surrendered to the Syrians. (R/D)

---

[1] Augustine claimed the Ottoman made his back hurt, and there was nowhere for friends to sleep if they were staying over.

P

Pacamac, The The pacamac was in vogue in the 1960s. The precursor to the cagoule, it consisted of a large sheet of brightly coloured polythene, cut and moulded into the shape of a coat, pliable enough to fold very small so you could keep it handily in your case and if it rained you could pull it out, put it on and spend the duration of the shower looking like a Durex Fiesta. The pacamac had two drawbacks. First, it wasn't waterproof, and second, it made you sweat so much there was no point in wearing it in the first place. The modern equivalent of pacamac wearers are people who wear transparent plastic raincoats with transparent hoods, obviously with the sole intention of imitating a large packet of crisps.

Pancakes Early attempts at making pancakes were unsophisticated.

Parmesan Cheese that smells of vomit. (D)

Party I think it was on the Anne Nightingale show or some such shit, they had this thing about parties, and said 'If you know someone big and fat invite them along and they can act as your bouncer.' Jay*zus*. This has that ice insensitivity which, it seems, only the professional nice can pull off. Here's the scenario if you follow that advice:

1. Fat boy gets party invite.
2. Fat boy delighted. No one ever invites him to parties and he didn't think you liked him. But it seems you did.
3. Fat boy arrives at party, is told to stand by the door for a bit and supposes that this is just something that every male invitee is doing in turn. This is, he supposes, what happens at parties. (He doesn't, after all, want to make it look like he doesn't go to a lot of parties.)
4. Everyone else goes off and dances.
5. Tooled-up rock hard twenty eight year olds walking past hear music and want to get in.
6. Fat screaming thirteen year old mess of snot, blood and tears with a broken nose and cut eye, comes up to you shouting 'Amanda says you only invited me because I'm fat and you wanted a bouncer! I hate you! Anyway, it's a disease – waaaaah!!' (R)

Penal System The first thing to say about the Penal System is that it sounds a little bit like the Penis System, which is a package you can buy in *Forum* magazine, including Dr Chartham's Vacuum Developer, a can of Stud Stay-Harder Spray, and a season ticket to Rob Newman's live show. However, we shall not be resorting to the Penal/Penis pun again, unless we run out of ideas.

The Penis Reform Bill of 1834 was brought by Elizabeth Fry as a Private Member's Bill in an attempt to bring the private members of most

104

Englishmen into line with one she encountered on the body of Mehmet Ali, a carpet trader in Istanbul. Hence the phrase 'Fry's Turkish Delight' (*See* Appendix A). (D/R)

Penis I have never seen another man's penis but no doubt they are all about the same size. So, the average male penis is twelve inches long and six inches in diameter. (R) (That's R)

Penis, David Baddiel Has a Very Big Yes, I have. (Not D)

Perchery You may well ask. In supermarkets nowadays (specifically Safeways, Peckham – S), you find that written on the lids of egg-boxes are the words 'Laid by Hens in the Safety of a Perchery'. No one knows what this means, or indeed, who in the egg industry imagined that it would increase sales of pullet-ovules to inform the potential consumer that the ovules in question have been Laid by Hens in the Safety of a Perchery.

Questions leap to mind:

1.*Why specify hens?* Surely, even the most biologically ignorant shopper is aware that the eggs are unlikely to have been laid by cocks, no matter how safe the environment. Or is there a sinister new breed of hermaphrodite chicken? And if so, is this why the hens have been removed to the safety of a perchery?

2.*Why 'safety'?* What danger is the average chicken likely to be in? Severe discomfort, yes, in the case of battery hens – but the entire defence of the battery-farmer is that his birds are completely safe. So what is the danger, that has required the hens to be removed to the safety of a perchery? Is it the danger of being strangled and given a Paxo-enema? This would not affect the egg-laying capacity of a chicken, unless it had developed strange, clairvoyant powers of

seeing into the future. Obviously, if chickens knew they were going to end up sliced and covered in Bisto, this might give them psychological problems. But there is no evidence of any Uri Geller-like powers in the fowl world.

Whatever the danger is, it seems that apparently, a perchery is the place to be. For years we've been led to believe that free-range is best; that hens are happiest strutting round a farmyard pecking at corn and doing rustic things. But no. Apparently, the place to find the well-adjusted, worry-free fowl is in a perchery – because a perchery is 'safe'. Possibly a perchery is equipped with handrails, illuminated exit-signs, fire-resistant straw, etc.

3.*What on earth is a perchery?* The average person, if asked where hens live, would probably say 'a henhouse'. Etymologically speaking, 'perchery' is not a difficult one to work out. A perchery is somewhere you perch. So, does this mean that a perchery has more room than a henhouse? Or maybe, the copywriter responsible for wording the egg-box lid simply wasn't satisfied with 'Laid by Hens in the Safety of a Henhouse'. So he opted for 'perchery' which sounds more like some sort of fish-farm. A perchery is obviously some sort of luxury hen-house – a sort of Docklands condo for chickens, perhaps with multi-gym, 24-hour porterage, and exorbitant service-charge.

However, the emphasis on perching seems odd. Perching implies something to perch on, and that suggests an alarming distance for the egg to drop. Surely, any bird who laid an egg while on a perch would find the egg smashed on the ground. So possibly a perchery is not somewhere where you perch, but somewhere where you can perch, somewhere where the perching option is available if you're not laying eggs. After the strain of producing another size 3, the bird can wander off to another corner of the perchery and have a perch. This still doesn't seem to have

A Henhouse

A Perchery

much to do with safety, but presumably 'Laid by Hens in the Comparative Comfort of a Perchery' wouldn't fit on the lid.

So – what is the overall impression one gains from Laid by Hens in the Safety of a Perchery? First, one is reassured that the eggs come from hens, and that one isn't going to go through the checkout with six chaffinch or herring-gull eggs by mistake. Second, one is informed that the eggs were laid in safety. One glances at all the other eggs on the shelf and imagines the hazardous conditions under which they were extruded; harassed hens trying their best to lay while trees fall, cars crash, and roofs collapse around them. And one purchases the safely-laid variety, lest such traumas should lead to a sub-standard product.

Perhaps this technique should be extended to other products – cheese could be 'Sucked Out of Cows in the Security of a Milking-Shed', sausages could be 'Torn off the Bones of Pigs in the Luxury of an Abattoir', etc. (S)

Pessimism And if I have a child, he will be born horrifically deformed, but, after much hard work and encouragement, will overcome his disabilities to become a serial killer. (R)

Pizza Posh cheese on toast.

PIZZA HUT; Make every pizza freshly to your order

Plate Tectonics Although it may seem solidly built the Earth's crust is basically a jerry-built botch of a job that no structural surveyor would pass if you applied for a mortgage on it. The whole thing is damp, subject to subsidence and without effective building guarantees. Furthermore it has proved almost impossible to trace the bloke who built it in the first place. Anyway, this rather poor analogy with its inference to the ultimate futility of Godhead isn't going to help us explain Plate Tectonics. For this purpose it is rather more productive to think of the world as a giant, cracked Creme Egg, except, of course, that the surface is made of rock not chocolate, it doesn't have a silver foil wrapping and it's best not to take a bite because instead of that really sickly yellow and white stuff, you'll get a gob of molten magma. So let's abandon analogy and find a better way of explaining it. Right. Basically the surface of the world is really cracked and the bits between the cracks are called plates. These all float around on a sea of molten magma and occasionally crash into each other with rather serious consequences like earthquakes, tidal waves and volcanic eruptions. If they hit each other really hard, they can even cause mountain ranges to be formed. It is therefore quite dangerous to live near the edges of these plates. Let's face it, it wouldn't be very nice to have your house forcibly moved to the top of a newly formed mountain, to do some unscheduled surfing or find yourself pot-holing when all you wanted to do was sit down with a good book and a cup of tea. High-risk areas include San Francisco, the Philippines and Japan. People live in these places because they are mad.

Britain is largely unaffected by such worries, which is a pity because it might have been a good way of getting rid of Essex (See ESSEX: MOST HORRID COUNTY IN BRITAIN). It also means that on a global scale British mountains are pathetic, Snowdon and Ben Nevis being roughly the same

A power cut

height as the speed humps they install on Swiss roads to slow down traffic. (H)

Plop Childish name for excrement based on the noise the stool makes when hitting the water in the toilet bowl. (D)

Pool, Swimming Place that's completely different when you go to it than when you see it on TV. You don't hear Ron Pickering saying[1] 'And Moorhouse is ahead, he's racing for the gold, and as they come up to the line – oh! he won't touch it because he's spotted a corn plaster floating in the irrigation channel. Meanwhile, Matt Biondi is coming up behind him with a polystyrene board, Biondi who's got a lot of work to do after he lost ten seconds at the start chucking his locker key in, diving in after it, and chucking it in again. And now he's coming up to the finishing line, but oh – his way's been blocked by some Pakistani children doing slow-motion Kung Fu in the shallow end. And now it would be over to the men's Olympic diving, but of course as usual the boards are roped off.' (R/D)

Power Cuts Very popular in the 1970s. Responsible for the fall of the Ted Heath Government, the rise of monetarism and lots of children with roughly the same birthday.

Psychology Study of loonies.

OEDIPUS COMPLEX

Famous psychological concept, but clearly not thought through. I mean, I don't want to shag my mother. Even my dad doesn't want to shag my mother. Even Rob Newman wouldn't want to shag my mother.

Men just don't fancy their mums, not even subconsciously. For a start, mums tend to be only just about female and only qualify for that by a whisker, normally on their chin. And if it was true that men secretly desire their mothers, then the girl at a party who was most successful at attracting a boy wouldn't be the one who dresses best, or dances best, but the one who wets a tissue with her own spittle and cleans round his mouth with it.

Moreover, the Oedipus myth itself revolves around someone called Jocasta. Someone called Jocasta is clearly not your mum. If anything it sounds like one of those made-up names from *Razzle* (*See* Appendix B). If the woman in *Oedipus Rex* had really been your mum, she'd have been called Maureen, or Pauline, or Mrs Beryl

---

[1] You don't hear Ron Pickering saying anything anymore, of course.

Thompson, and Sophocles would have had to rethink the final scene:

OEDIPUS:
Oh, woe, wife-mother both! Know that we
Have defiled every human sacrament. See
How my eyes bleed, for I have stabbed them
Out.

MRS BERYL THOMPSON:
    Yes, well you just wait on the mat until
I've put some paper down.

OEDIPUS:
              But what in heaven
and earth can help us
With this mortal tragedy?

MRS BERYL THOMPSON:
              Hm. Let me see. I
Know.

(SHE PICKS UP A QUILL AND SOME BASILDON BOND AND BEGINS TO WRITE)

    Dear Katie Boyle.
For some time it appears that I have been
Unknowingly sleeping with my own son.
What should I do? Yours Beryl Thompson (Mrs).

P.S. A handy tip in the kitchen is
Always put some paper down.

REPRESSION

The sort of sub-hippies who live by a kind of idiot's Freud are often convinced that if you express an intense dislike for something, that indicates a deeply repressed desire to have it. This suggests that the whole country wants to gang-bang Michael Barrymore. This theory is most often used to allege repressed homosexuality. Now, I don't mind some other man giving me an affectionate slap on the back — as long as I have at least three months' written notice — but just because I might complain when some reconstructed man ostentatiously demonstrates his lack of homophobia by sticking his tongue in my ear, it doesn't mean that next week, once I've come to terms with it, I'm off on a camping holiday with the singer from Erasure.

DREAMS

Dreams are not wish-fulfilment. I do not secretly want Leslie Crowther to barge into my old German teacher's class on stilts shouting 'This way for hovercraft!' (D/R)

Pub, The In 1979 Sham 69 sang 'We're going down the pub.' What of course they should have sung was 'We're going down that place where the tables are all wet, the toilets don't work, and you have to wait hours to get on the pool table for the privilege of watching the bloke who's been on it all night clear up after his first break.' The pub is a rubbish place: at its very best, it's about as good as a bad evening at home, except it costs more and you can't hear the telly.

But perhaps the most rubbish thing about the pub is the 'choice' it offers between the saloon and the public bar. What sort of choice is that? 'Oh let me see now . . . either I can go into the saloon bar . . . or I can go into that bit where there's no carpet, no ashtrays, and no women, and spend the evening explaining to some old bastard with a knife that it wasn't me who slept with his wife in 1964.' In fact, however, the public bar is where logically you should go, as going to the pub is itself a masochistic act. If you were pushed for time, but still wanted to enjoy the whole pub experience in one go, you could always ask the barman for an emetic and a head-butt — although, if you were to do it properly, you'd still have to wait half an hour to catch his eye.

Of course, though, pubs do have the most marvellous in-house entertainment: if not someone who looks like your mum taking her clothes off, it's a jukebox which some bastard has programmed to play 'Freebird' all night, or a Gaelic band who continue to plough on through their fifty thinly-disguised musical tributes to the IRA, despite endless cries of 'Hi-ho Silver Lining!!' (R/D)

Puddings While everybody else has realised that puddings are too complicated and time-consuming to bother with, they are still made by old people. This is basically because during rationing they all went a bit crazy through being hungry a lot of the time and developed a theory that you should eat an awful lot of the food you could get hold of. Unfortunately for future generations there was very little soft scoop ice cream, yoghurt and fresh fruit that wasn't intercepted by the marauding German U-boats, while huge quantities of flour, lard, treacle, jam and custard did manage to break through the vice-like grip on our trade lines. This tradition has therefore survived and the argument that Marks and Spencer now has products that are much better for you in plentiful supply holds little sway with someone who lived through this period. As a result it is still impossible to leave the home of an elderly relative without feeling so full that one more mouthful would be certain death.

Puddings That Sound Rude *Melon* (not that rude), *Spotted Dick* (quite rude) and *Throbbing Donger* (which would be very rude but unfortunately does not exist).

Puddings That You Ate At School But Haven't Had Since *Tapioca, Semolina* with a blob of strawberry jam in the middle, and something called *Foam Rubber* which was like a sort of mousse with fluorescent colouring that used to come in slabs and make you feel really sick.

Puddings Which Aren't Really Puddings In The Accepted Sense *Black Pudding* does not taste very nice with custard.

Puffenstuff, H.R. A children's programme so obscure I don't know why I've bothered to write it down. (H)

Punt, Steve The rightful King of Norway, Steve has spent most of his adult life in a single-minded struggle to convince the Norwegian parliament of his right to wield constitutional power. Traces his ancestral line back to Olaf the Belligerent (AD 718–63) and is directly descended through Prince Jorvik II, who formed part of a Viking invasion party in the ninth century. While the rest pillaged and looted an area roughly equivalent to today's Hull, Jorvik got a bit lost and missed the boat back to Stavanger. His descendants have always lived in England ever since. Although of Norwegian royal blood, Steve has never actually been to Norway and can never remember the name of its capital, getting it mixed up with Finland's. He cannot speak a word of Norwegian, so if he ever came to the throne, he would have to address his subjects via a phrase book. Despite this, he is very proud of his royal blood, and often uses it to impress women, viz. 'I am the rightful King of Norway. Do you want to come to the pictures?'

Purves, Peter Presenter who never really found his *métier* after leaving *Blue Peter*. Perhaps best known in recent years for his appearance in the National Power advert during the World Cup in which he strode onto a pitch to ask if we'd ever wondered about where all the power comes from that's powering the floodlights right now.

In accepting this advert, Purves earned . . . £20,000? £30,000? But at the same time, he became the most hated man in the entire country. Appearing in every single advert break in ITV's coverage, the National Power advert intruded so much on the consciousness that any viewer of Italia '90 lived in fear of the following scenario:

JOHN MOTSON: Sarajevic . . . to the

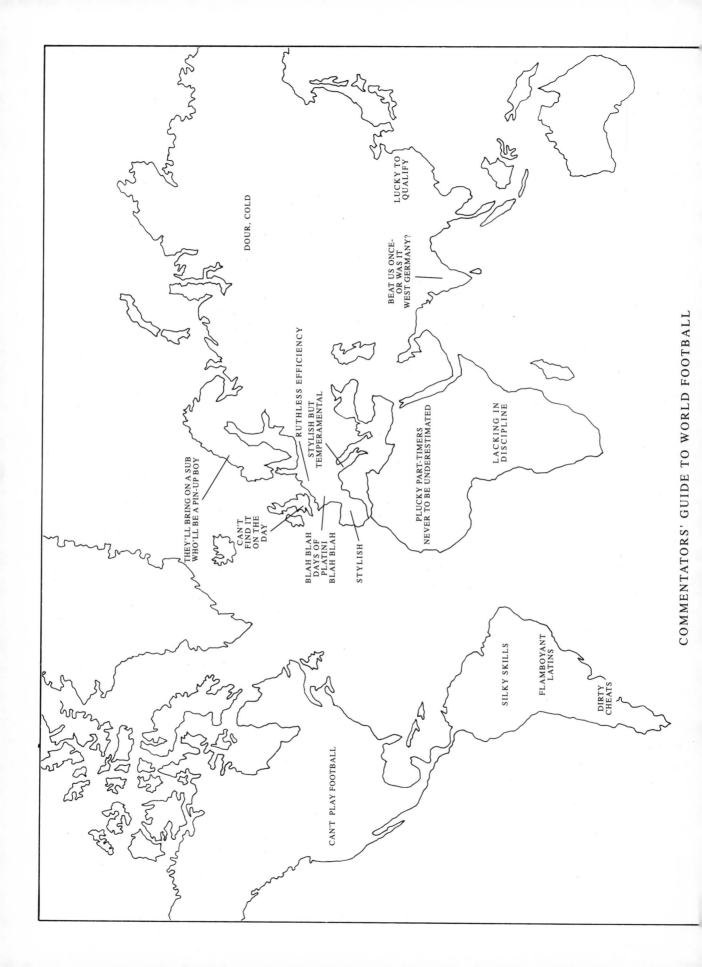

COMMENTATORS' GUIDE TO WORLD FOOTBALL

Yugoslav No. 10 . . . er . . . (*desperate rustling of paper*) . . . er . . . Stoykovic. Maradonna coming to intercept . . . but hold on a minute! A man in a suit has strode purposefully on to the pitch! He's about fifty, with a full head of grey hair, but in the same style as it used to be when it was dark.

PETER PURVES: Maradonna – have you ever wondered what power it is that's driving these floodlights right now?

MARADONNA: Quiere usted de cielo unmujer Valerie Singleton elephant shit all over the floor?

PETER PURVES: And you, Dragon Stoykovic, have you ever wondered how it is that I've managed to come up with an idea even more shite than *Kick Start*?

And second, in a world cup game, who on earth does wonder where all the power comes from?

JOHN MOTSON: Well, here we go, it's the most important penalty kick for an England team for twenty five years, Chris Waddle is just about to take it, a last word, Ray Wilkins?

(Short pause)

RAY WILKINS: Oh, sorry John, I was miles away. I was wondering where all the power comes from that drives all the electricity in England and Wales.

JOHN MOTSON: Oh that's a good question, I don't know. National Grid?

(A huge anguished cry as Waddle boots it over the top Oh God Oh God)

RAY: Maybe, but that would only account for about 42 per cent of the total . . .

(R/D)

Pushkin, Leonid Russian poet and thinker who stunned the world by choosing to call his autobiography *Oh No, It's Leonid Pushkin!* after he saw the Granada sitcom about Selwyn Froggit. (R/D)

Leonid Pushkin

Pyramids The last remaining wonder of the Ancient World. A spectacular feat of engineering and imagination whose unique minty taste inspired the creation of the Cadbury's Pyramint.

Pyramint Chocolate in the shape of a pyramid with a minty bit roughly where the burial chamber would be.

Quark Sub-atomic particle. There's all sorts of the little buggers – strange quarks, charmed quarks, and quarks with spin on them. There's also a sort of cheesy spread called *Quark,* which just shows that if you want to attract the modern supermarket consumer to a dairy product, you should find a brand name which conjures up an image of particle accelerators and high-speed proton collisions.

Queen Freddie Mercury, Brian May, Roger Taylor, and the other bloke. Brian May is now shacked up with Anita Dobson, and working on a single called 'Anyone Can Fall in Thunderbolt and Lightning, Very Very Frightening Indeed'.

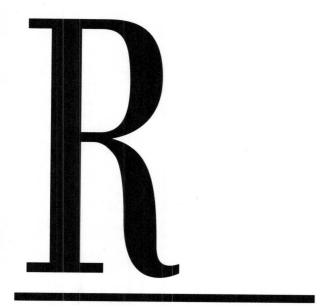

R

Radio Invented by Marconi, developed by the British, shrunk by the Japanese (*See* THE ONLY GOOD JOKE IN STEVEN SPIELBERG'S *1941*) and knocked into the bath by me.

Radio Comedy, The Golden Age of The golden age of radio comedy can best be summed up in one phrase: 'Can you hear me, muther!' This was considered such a funny thing to say in the 1930s that there was a show called *Can You Hear Me, Muther!* which began every week with the unmistakable voice of Jack Hulbert shouting 'Can you hear me, muther!', and then continued for three and a half hours with him shouting it again and again and again. Jack was, of course, teamed up with legendary 'Whistling' Arthur Hackton, loved all over the country for his famous catchphrase 'Please don't throw bottles, I'm a haemophiliac.' *Can You Hear Me, Muther!* or *CYHMM*, as it soon became known, set the format for all the best comedy shows of the pre-war period – *The 'Can You Hear Me, Muther!' Roadshow, Muther? Can You Hear Me?* and, of course, the hilarious *Is The Bloody Woman Deaf?* But then suddenly, and irreversibly, radio comedy underwent a revolution when in 1935, the unforgettable tones of Arthur Spilton introduced *Can You Hear Me, Futher!*

Arthur and the other members of the *Can You Hear Me, Futher!* team – Jack Hargreaves, Norman Littlewood and 'Funny' Johnny Clydemouth – enjoyed an unprecedented run of 153 series on the BBC before, tragically, they all died of a simultaneous heart attack in June 1938. But their basic job of bringing happiness to millions during the harsh inter-war years had been done, as Doris Fishwick records in her autobiography, *My Cunt's an Open Book:* 'all the family used to gather round the crackling radio and laugh – oh, how we laughed – as it melted away on the bonfire.'

And then came war once more. Hitler, unable

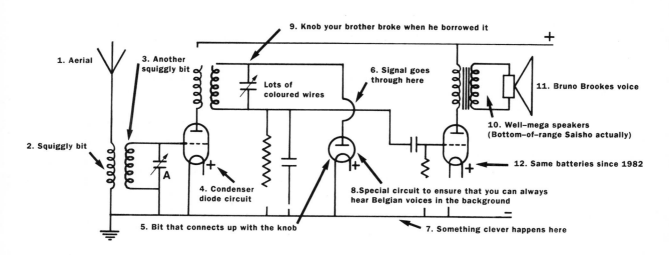

How a radio works

1. Aerial
2. Squiggly bit
3. Another squiggly bit
4. Condenser diode circuit
5. Bit that connects up with the knob
6. Signal goes through here
7. Something clever happens here
8. Special circuit to ensure that you can always hear Belgian voices in the background
9. Knob your brother broke when he borrowed it
10. Well–mega speakers (Bottom–of–range Saisho actually)
11. Bruno Brookes voice
12. Same batteries since 1982

Lots of coloured wires

to bear continued repeats of *Can You Hear Me, Futher!* on the World Service, invaded Poland. During the dark days of the Blitz, perhaps only one hope sustained the British people. Star of the music halls, Tommy Tucker would come on the radio every night and satirise the German war-effort to a pulp with quips like 'What about that old Hitler fella, eh? I wouldn't buy any tomatoes off him!' and 'What about Goebbels, eh? Sounds like a raving hamster!' Then of course he would sing his song:

> *Oh those nasty bloomin' Nazis*
> *They don't come down our way*
> *But I can tell you if one did*
> *Then this is what I'd say!*
>
> *I'd say 'Iddly-diddly pom pom pom*
> *Shilly shally shoo*
> *Run tun tun tun tun tun*
> *Knicky knacky noo!'*

Yes, the hope that sustained the British people during the dark days of the Blitz was that a bomb might fall on Tommy Tucker's house. (D/R)

Railways Everyone's always on about how French and German railways are much better than ours, but these people have obviously never travelled on French and German railways, because if they had, they'd know it was rubbish. The fact is that despite greater public subsidy and higher investment, French and German railways have a major problem – no matter how far in advance you reserve your seat *you will always find it occupied by a fat Belgian who speaks no English*. This means having to stand from Boulogne-Maritime to Milan, with only the 589 other British Inter-railing cheapskates to talk to.

Railway Timetables The problem with these is that they are almost impossible to understand and don't reflect the realities of the service. An accurate rail timetable would read

Manchester → The Midlands – London

MONDAYS TO SATURDAYS

		IC s MO A	IC s MX A	IC s X B	IC s P B	IC s P B	IC s P B	IC R s MO C D
Manchester Piccadilly	d	0030	0030	0600	0705	0725	0740	0823
Stockport	d	0044	0044	0608	0713	0733	0752	0824
Woken by Ticket Collector	d	0045	0045	0609	0714	0734	0753	0825
Macclesfield	d	——	——	——	——	——	——	0933
Massive Queue at Buffet	d	0045	0045	0612	——	0800	——	——
Wilmslow	d	——	——	——	——	0844	——	——
Incomprehensible Announcement	d	0213	0213	0800	0745	0900	0923	1015
Buffet Runs Out of Hot Water	d	0215	——	——	0800	——	——	——
Nuneaton	d	0335	0311	——	——	——	——	——
Engine Breaks Down	d	——	0320	0900	——	——	——	1110
Rugby	a	0345	0337	0930	——	——	——	——
Buffet Runs Out of Penguins	a	0345	0400	1015	——	——	1023	1215
Milton Keynes	a	0426	0419	——	——	——	1032	——
Buffet Runs Out of Everything Else	a	0435	——	1100	——	1000	1045	——
Long Wait for No Reason	a	0436	——	1110	——	1100	1054	1320
Argue with Guard	a	0436	——	1130	——	——	1100	——
Watford Junction	a	——	——	——	——	——	1134	——
Unexplained Delay 200yds from Terminus	a	0500	0510	1145	0902	1205	1114	1400
London Euston	a	0528	0517	1200	0928	1723	1217	1600
Can't get a Taxi	d	——	——	——	——	1130	1215	1435

SUNDAYS

		IC	IC	IC	IC	IC	IC	IC
Manchester Piccadilly	d	——	——	——	——	1115	——	——
Delay for Engineering Work	d	——	——	——	——	1230	——	——
Norwich	d	——	——	——	1100	1750	——	——
Realise there is No Buffet	d	——	0900	——	1400	——	——	——
Macclesfield	d	——	——	——	——	——	——	——
Air Vents Permanently on Hot	d	——	——	——	——	1751	——	——
Man Next to You Keeps Farting	d	——	——	——	——	1804	——	——
Wilmslow	d	——	——	——	——	1900	——	——
Hartlepool	d	——	——	——	——	2104	——	——
Dumfries	d	——	——	——	——	0203	——	——
Baby Screaming Continuously	d	0913	——	——	——	0400	——	——
Lincoln	d	——	——	——	——	0530	——	——
Where on Earth Are We Now	d	——	——	——	——	0545	——	——
Watford Junction	d	——	——	——	——	0745	——	——
London Euston	d	——	——	——	——	——	——	1145

General Notes

IC   Intercity train with;
– big seats for those with more money than sense (or whose companies are paying)
– slightly crappier seats for the rest of you.

☕   Buffet Service with tea, coffee, snacks and toasted sandwiches all of which are impossible to carry back to your seat if the train is moving.

R   Completely random train times.

Ω   Man with irritating Walkman.

☎   Lots of wankers with Vodaphones.

⚲   Urine all over the toilet seat.

🚻   Even though we've charged you £50 you can't sit down.

CD   Change for Didcot at Swindon. If you seriously want to go to Swindon, that is. This service does not operate on alternate Tuesdays.

🚃   Very old, dilapidated Rolling Stock that we only use on Sundays.

◊   Sleeper Cabins may be occupied until 0700, but you will be woken at 0530 by a very grumpy guard who will bash on your door, shout at you to get up, and then try to force feed you with a cup of luke warm tea and an individual slab of Walkers Shortcake.

A   Outward Supersaver ticket holders may **NOT** travel on this train to Milton Keynes, Watford or London. Inward Supersaver ticket holders may **NOT** travel on this service if they boarded north of Norwich on a Thursday afternoon in June, Saturday evening in February or any lunchtime during the daylight saving period. In this case, excess fares will be payable to the approved representative of The British Railways Board, with the exception of those in receipt of a valid railcard purchased on or before the proposed Intercity fare increase and provided that the cardholder is not, nor has ever been, a member of Her Majesty's Armed Forces, a pensioner, or understands that this pricing policy is a rip off.

Reigate Market town in East Surrey. Mentioned in the 'Domesday Book' as 'Churchfelle', situated below the North Downs at the crossroads of the London–South Coast route and the east–west path known as the Pilgrim's Way. *The Green Lion Pub,* in the town centre, was originally a tavern where pilgrims would spent a night on their way to Canterbury. Nowadays it is chiefly known for under-age drinking. On a Friday night you might see a fight. The visitor should not miss a trip around the town's *One-Way System.* A typical early 1970s design, this feeds the motorists around Castlefield Road, past the Town Hall and then into West Street. On the left here you can see *Andrew Glass the Stationer* and *Perfect Pizza.* Make sure you stop at the traffic lights at the junction with Bell Street; here, the visitor has a fine view of the *Alliance and Leicester Building Society.* For the more adventurous, you can turn left into Bancroft Road, where the delights of the *Library* and the *Screen at Reigate* await.

Put aside at least ten minutes to savour the full delights of the *High Street.* Here, a bewildering variety of shops tempt the visitor, including *Boots, Marks and Spencers Food Hall* and *The Art of Living.* No visit to Reigate is complete without a trip to the *Priory Car Park,* a large tarmac expanse, cleverly decorated with white lines arranged in grids to help the motorists align their vehicles. Do not be frightened off by the *Ticket Machines* – they are simple to operate and 20p is a small price to pay for an hour in one of East Surrey's most delightful spots.

For an afternoon excursion, venture north through the *Castle Grounds.* Here you can see the ruined gatehouse of *Reigate Castle,* demolished by the victorious Cromwell after the Civil War. Cross the road and you will walk north and you can see, on your right, the unmistakable skyline of *Texas Homecare.* Beyond this is the *Railway Station,* where, if you wait for a short while, you may see the railway crossing in action. This fas-

cinating ceremony, in which two metal barriers are lowered blocking the A217 in both directions, takes place half-hourly and is not to be missed.

Anwar Sadat

If you really want to experience Reigate to its fullest, hire a car and venture out of town. Attractions include the *East Surrey Hospital, Reigate Heath Windmill* (which used to work) and, of course, *Junction 7 of the M25.*

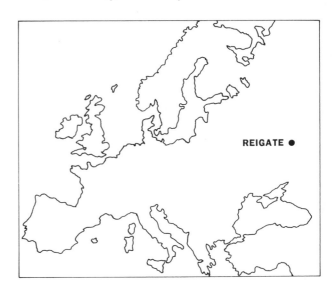

Remington Fuzz-Away and Nose Hair Clipper

Perhaps the most useful thing invented in the twentieth century.

Sales The January sales are the biggest rip off in the calendar. For a start they begin on 27 December, so the shops can rub in the fact that you had to pay full price for the same stuff three days earlier. Second, the stuff which is in the sale is never the stuff you want. A record shop, for example, will say 'Records and Tapes from 99p', but in fact what's on sale for 99p will be:

Joe Dolce
Frampton Comes Alive!
The second Sade album
Brotherhood of Man
Baccarra
Glenn Medeiros
The soundtrack album of Can't Stop The Music
Anything by Rick Astley.

Also, beware the small print on sale price items. If you find an album called

A tribute to ELVIS by Edward Nobhead and the Craptones

look closely, because it's probably called

A tribute to ELVIS by Edward Nobhead and the Craptones

The only shops worth going to for sales are the ones which sell a range of discounted rubbish. That is to say department stores. However department stores also have their drawbacks. For a start there are certain words that only survive in the English language through department stores – words like 'haberdashery'. People in real life don't go round saying 'Mmm . . . I do like your haberdashery!' or 'I suppose you'll want some millinery for your birthday'. The language of department stores exists nowhere else, which is probably just as well. We can only hope that other people do not start trying to speak in Department-Store-ese:

GANG GRAB GOODS @ 100% OFF

Police today are hunting three men who robbed a bank in Ealing, getting away with 1/4 million pounds. The gang, who had all disguised their faces with haberdashery and lingerie, were all wearing menswear. One of them was also wearing a toilet requisite and a large millinery item. They threatened the staff with a sawn-off wildlife termination requisite, before making off. Police are currently using a large amount of stationery and electrical goods to trace the men although they say that at least two of them are already known to their records department.

Sam Brown Syndrome She looks a bit like her dad. And I couldn't shag her for fear that, at the moment of orgasm, I'd see Joe Brown's smiling face singing 'I'm Enery the VIIIth I Am'. This is sometimes known as the 'Janet Jackson Syndrome' if someone looks too much like their brother for ontological comfort. (R)

Satire, History Of The great social impact of satire can be gauged from the example of Ernst Von Muller, the legendary German stand-up comedian, who in Munich in 1939 performed

Stalin

Stalin after a glass of milk

his devastatingly effective piece 'Hitler is Crap'. Soon afterwards, Ernst went on to take satire into variety with a disappearing act, which proved so successful that he wasn't seen again until the liberation of Birkenau in 1945.

Stalin was another great dictator who reeled under satirical attack. Trotsky, in particular, used to enrage Stalin with wickedly inventive gibes on the problems of having a large moustache. 'Social structures may come and go', Trotsky claimed in *Literature and Revolution*, 'but Joe Stalin cannot finish a glass of milk without looking like a zebra crossing.'

Stalin, however, was to have the last laugh, when an ice pick was slammed into Trotsky's skull – still possibly the most effective heckle in the history of comedy.

The golden age of satire was, of course, the eighteenth century, and in particular the works of Alexander Pope:

> 'Has not Colley still his lord and whore,
> His butcher's Henley? His freemason's Moore?
> Does not one table Bavius still admit?
> Still to one Bishop Philips seem a wit?'

(Alexander Pope, *The Rape of The Lock*, 1089–93)

Now, although it's very difficult for the modern reader to understand these lines, we must remember that for the eighteenth century reader, it was completely impossible, as most of the jokes refer to Pope's landlady, Jonathan's Swift's inability to waltz, and Bavius, his pen pal in Czechoslovakia, whom Pope suspected of only corresponding with him because he wanted somewhere to stay when he came to England.
(R/D)

Scargill, Arthur Man who thinks he looks all right with a haircut which, if a hairdresser had given it to The Elephant Man, The Elephant Man would have said 'I look awful.' Much of the money donated to the NUM during the 1985 miners' strike came, in fact, not from people sympathetic to the miners' cause, but just from people feeling sorry for a man who they assumed had some medical reason to wear a wire wool wig.

If it is a wig, that may explain other anomalies surrounding the strike. The reason he continued the strike long after defeat was a certainty may have been simply to carry on wearing the baseball cap. Also, it may explain some of the confusing minutes of NUM strike committee meetings:

```
Strike Committee Meeting,
         12.6.85.


Comrade Walsh rose to make
the point that the meeting
could not commence until
someone complimented Comrade
Scargill on how shiny, lus-
trous and full-bodied his
hair was. At this point,
Comrade    Laurence    said,
'Arthur? Good God. I thought
it was Farrah Fawcett-
Majors.'
   Meeting Adjourned.
```

(R/D)

School Schools have long been a prime source of literary inspiration, but usually, in the books, sordid realities were glossed over; otherwise, it would all have looked very different:

'Grooooh!'

Bunter groaned! The Fat Owl of the Remove was diddled and dished. Quelch was on the war-path!

'Ooooooh!' groaned Bunter.

'Stop that infernal din,' said Bob Cherry, dumping his soccer boots in the corner of the study. 'Whatever can be the matter,to make you howl like that, you frabjous ass?'

Bunter looked balefully at him through his little round spectacles.

'I got a letter from Bunter Court this morning,' he explained.

'So?' said Harry Wharton, buttering a freshly-toasted muffin. 'Chaps get letters every day. Your pater refusing to give you yur allowance, you fat frump?'

'Mater and pater are separating,' explained Bunter. 'Pater has got our chambermaid pregnant. I say, you fellows - I'm in a terrible psychological trauma.'

'The traumafulness of the psychology is terrific,' murmured Hurree Jamset Ram Singh.

'Don't get in a spin,' put in Lord Mauleverer. 'One of the chaps in the Shell was gettin' through a quarter of dope a day. Gigglin' all through prep, what? Turned out he was only doin' it to get over his sexual obsession with Matron.'

'Well, dash it all,' shouted Bob Cherry, 'she is the only female within ten miles, Mauly!'

'Don't need to tell me,' said Mauleverer, languidly. 'I was wankin' only this mornin'.'

'The frustratedness is terrific,' murmured the Nabob of Bhaniphur.

'Cave!' whispered Harry Wharton.

'Oh crikey!'

It was Quelch! He strode into the room, his gimlet-eye glinting like a gimlet. He stared at each boy in turn.

'Bunter!' he bellowed.

'Oh crikey!' stammered the Owl. 'I. . . er. . .'

'Bunter!' cried Quelch.

'Y-y-y. . .yes,sir!'

'You get unmercifully bullied for being overweight, don't you?'

'Y-y-yes, sir.'

'That's because most of the boys in this school are crypto-fascists, Bunter.'

'Y-y-yes, sir.'

'Have you ever had homosexual relations, Bunter?'

'Y-y-yes, sir! I mean, no sir!' What was it Skinner had said to him as they changed for cricket?

'If I discover any of the Remove indulging in homosexual practices, I shall slipper the lot of you!'

'None of us are queers, sir!' piped up Bob Cherry. 'Why, Wharton got a girl from the village in the family way only last week.'

'Silly girl wanted me to marry her,' growled Wharton. 'Common little trollope, as well. Told her to see matron.'

'The hypocriticalness of the class system is terrific,' said Hurree Jamset Ram Singh, in a rather self-aware way. 'The sterility of the atmosphere is the unnaturalness of the British temperament, as Orwell says. . . .'

'Don't mention that communist in here!' shouted Bob Cherry. 'Hitler's got the right idea about people like him!'

'Don't be so sure, Cherry,' said Mauleverer, crossing his elegant legs. 'I'm thinkin' of spyin' for the Russians, you know. If I get into Cambridge, that is.'

Morning assembly is an integral part of public school life

Public schools formed the basis of almost all school stories until recently. There are many famous fictional school characters who would have no idea what to make of the modern world:

NATIONAL ASSESSMENT TESTS AT ST. CUSTARDS

'Coo er gosh' sa my grate friend peason as he STARE BLANKLY at paper in front of him. 'Have you seen this, molesworth?' he sa, litely.

'It is a National Assessment test, molesworth. we must all be tested for nationally-recognised standards of litteracy and numeracy.'

Chiz! Wot is this, i fume, but some further piece of beaurocratic meddling and polittical interference in the running of our skools? We are mere guinea pigs, especially molesworth 2 who look more like the abovementioned than most hem hem.

'wot are we diskussing?' cri a gurly voice. 'Poetry? botany? Last night's Late Show?' it is fotherington-thomas chiz he is utterly wet and a weed.

'We are diskussing Spurs' chances in Europe' i reply, knoing this will get rid of him. he is utterly wet and a weed and he go off to fill in his application form for BBC Production Trainee which he will fail to get for the eighth time.

'Wot can we do?' sa peason. 'We cannot take National Assessment tests molesworth we shall score 0 and hav to have extra lesons with Sigismund the mad maths naster.'

'But he is hopless,' i replie. 'he only kno how to work out how long it take to run a bath 150 cm long by 40 cm high.' Also he is a TEECHER chiz so he hav 0 money and hav to work out his overdraft by algebra cheers cheers. St custards is low on funds hem hem and when fotherington-thomas sa 'hullo clouds hullo sky' he is looking through skool roof at the time.

Just then tall hansom figure appere it is Grabber captain of skool and winner of mrs joyful prize for rafia work.(he also smoke POT surreptitiously and hav a father who is doing porige for insider deeling cheers cheers.)

'Wot are you chaps diskussing?' he ask.

'The National Currilculum.' we sa.

'A typical piece of polittical expediency' he replie. 'Yet another example of britain's skoolchildren being used a fodder in social experimentation.'

My mind leap to molesworth 2 who look like he hav been used in experimentation of all kinds. 'Let us not condemn without knoing the full facts' i sa. (Coo er gosh posh eh? I have learnt this phrase from watching KWESTION TIME with Peter Scissors.) 'Let us hav a look.'

We look at the paper. It hav been complied by KENETH CLARKE Edducation Sekretary chiz and on it someone hav written all the things british skoolchidren are supposed to kno. It sa:

ENGLISH. Everyone should read SHAKESPEARE no one knos why he is utterly wet and a weed. the plas are written in POETRY which is sissy as any fule kno, and full of sex and violence it is worse than *Eastenders* hem hem. Also in SHAKESPEARE men dress up as women wot sort of example is this i ask you. It hav a bad influence. Especially on Mr Granbury the physics teacher enuff said. The matter is sub judice.

MATHS. The nat. Curriculum sa we should all kno about COMPUTERS come on i ask you no one at st. custard's knows from a mouse from a ram. (especially the skool cook). in fact, our arith. is so ppor perhaps we shall all get jobs doing econommic forecasts for the Treasury ho ho. (satire)

LANGWAGES. There are only three langwages – FRENCH which is a swiz and chiz. You can only use it in France and when you do the Fr. people laugh at you and reply in Eng. Then there is GERMAN which is unspeakable (litrally). finally there is LATIN which all tories think is good but generations of skoolchildren kno is aktually about as much use as the area of a rhombus. So wot if you can go around saing – 'Of course, "pontoon" is an interesting word because it comes from the Latin "pons, pontis" meaning a bridge.' If you go around talking like this people do not sa you are clever for knoing Lat they simply sa wot you aktually are i.e. a WANKER. enuff said.

SCIENCE. there is no point in st custard's teaching science well becos everyone kno the problem. if you are a swot at science and hav a grate brane then you will go to university and get yore degree and then you will leave and there will be no research place becos the government hav not given any grant. this mean you hav to go and work in AMERICA which is a swiz becos you will miss *neighbours* and *eastenders* etc. however you will be paid lots of money and get to meet GURLS like on BAYWATCH hem hem so maybe it is not such a bad idea after all. Pass the bunsen burner if molesworth 2 hav not eaten it.

SCHOOL: A typical inner-city comprehensive

7-Up Documentary series from which Rob Newman was rejected. Robbie tells: 'When we were seven, they took me and some other kids to a playground. The film-crew caught up with us every seven years for *14-Up* and *21-Up,* by which time the others had become jockeys, students or housewives. I was still trying to get to go on a roundabout. (R/D)

Shaw, George Bernard Shaw is remembered chiefly for the superhuman sacrifice he once made for the sake of an epigram. Lady Asquith had just come up trumps with: 'Mr Shaw, you and I should make love – with my looks and your brains we'd have great children.' To which Shaw replied: 'Aha, but what if it had my looks and your brains?' The remark was greeted with applause, but seconds later, having stepped through French windows into the dusk-garden, George was heard to shout: 'I've just blown out a definite shag! What a stupid fucking wanker!'

In his journal, present and napkinned eye-witness Jung attributes this epigram-first-think-later carry-on to Shaw's 'fear of sex'. A hypothesis he backs up by recording an oddly similar incident which occurred less than a week later. Mme Weil suggested that she and Shaw should have sex, because, as she put it, 'With my vagina and your dick it would be a great fuck.' To which Shaw replied, 'aha . . . but what if we had my vagina and your dick? . . . . Oh no, I've done it again!'

Other come-ons Shaw passed up:

COUNTESS IVANOVA: Oy George – fancy a shag?

SHAW: Fancy? It is the darling of society but the outcast of the spirit . . . . Oh, for fuck's sake!

PRINCESS FRIEDA: Mr Shaw, have you any thoughts on modern theatre?

SHAW: Rip my fucking clothes off and fuck me on the table, like the slut I am! . . . Oh dear. (R)

Shaw lines up another epigram, and eligible bachelors queue up for the rebound.

George Bernard Shaw about to not cop off.

Shellsuit The success of shellsuits is easily explained – they are shapeless and almost incredibly unflattering and, as such, form part of a British fashion tradition stretching back centuries. The shellsuit was originally a garment worn by sportsmen and women, but it is essential to remember that wearing a shellsuit *does not make you look sporty*. More often than not, it makes you look like an unfit fatty with no taste in clothes, who has been gullible enough to fork out ninety quid for a crinkly nylon sleeping-bag with legs.

Shellsuits, Families Wearing Matching See above x 4.

Shoes The best place for these is usually on your feet.

Two peasants stop for a shoe shine

Sicursiv A word that everyone has seen but no one can remember where. (We're not giving you any clues.)

Smiths, The (Smiths) Seminal 1980s band whose music was born out of the chemistry between its two central figures, Mike Joyce and Andy Rourke. The union of Joyce – quiet, tidy – with Rourke – captain of his local pub team – produced a series of songs more memorable for their drum and bass lines than for their intrusive guitar parts and sometimes silly lyrics. Since the band split in 1987, fans have argued which of the two was the more elemental: Joyce, with his habit of turning up to gigs in plenty of time with some sandwiches, or Rourke, with his ability to play the drums – or was it the bass? Rourke in particular inspired a cult of celibacy, due to his inability to get off with anyone (despite being in Smiths, The). (R/D)

Soap On A Rope A bar of soap with a large piece of string through it. It's only possible product benefit was that it rhymed. Surprisingly no longer with us.

Solzhenitsyn, Alexander A dissident Russian author primarily remembered for having a beard that sort of went under his chin like a strap, and

made his hair look like a hat.

Space Space exploration is crap. It's nothing like we were taught to expect from the TV (see below).

Space exploration has however provided us with one of the funniest names in history: Buzz Aldrin, which for sheer intergalactic silliness must rank with Undabanige Sotole, Tony Gubba, and Ken and Beryl Rosencrap.[1] There is no possible explanation for why Mr Aldrin should have been christened 'Buzz', although some have pointed the finger at his father, Ding-Dong Aldrin.

In the early 1960s, everyone thought that the first space launch was simply a two-horse race between the Russians and the Americans. So it must have been a terrible shock to them both when they were pipped to the post by a monkey. It has always been officially stated that none of the monkeys who went into space in the 1960s suffered any acquired remarkable qualities, although this is belied by a secret transcript *TMWE* discovered in the bin at Mission Control, Houston (See fig).

[1] Friends of Colin and Sarah Baddiel in the swinging Seventies, now remembered only through a mist of sideburns, wife swapping, and velvet curtains

TRANSCRIPT OF COMMUNICATION BETWEEN MISSION CONTROL AND APOLLO 2,   2.3.61, 08.43HRS

MISSION: HELLO, THIS IS HOUSTON...WE SEEM TO BE PICKING UP SOME TRANSMISSIONS FROM INSIDE THE MONKEY CABIN. HERE IT COMES AGAIN.

APOLLO: COEE DAD - THE PIANO'S ON ME FOOT!

APOLLO: CAN YOU RIDE TANDEM?

APOLLO: THERE'S NO OTHER TEA TO BEAT PG.

Stonecladding The technique of covering a house in large multicoloured blocks of pink and beige, because the owner believes that people will then say 'Oh look, one of the houses in that row of otherwise-identical urban properties is a rural cottage built of Cotswold stone', whereas in fact they will say 'Oh look, that person has had their perfectly attractive terraced house stoneclad . . . . how crap can you get.'

Stonehenge An enduring mystery.

HAT SEEMS ILLOGICAL, CAPTAIN.

STONEHENGE; Archaeologists still don't know what the fuck it was for.

129

Mike Joyce, Andy Rourke, and the other two.

Suburbs The dullest bit of any city. All suburbs have roads named after trees in an attempt to give them a spurious country atmosphere: Limes Avenue – because the plot of land had a lime tree on it before it was cut down to make way for the houses; Chestnut Road – because a building labourer found a conker in the foundations; and Acacia Avenue – because One Duff Birch Avenue doesn't sound very good and the planner understood the importance of alliteration.

Sugar Sugar is one of the fuels for life itself (The British Sugar Bureau) or a major hazard to both dental and arterio-sclerotic health (everyone else). However, none of this is as important as the fact that the upper classes are so cretinously unintelligent that they need a special tool to pick it up.

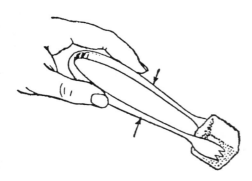

SUGAR; picking it up can be a problem

Supermarket The shrine of modern consumerism, but more importantly, a good place to look at people. People in supermarkets divide up into distinct types, who can be roughly delineated as follows:

1. *The Coronary Case* CCs are obviously heading for cardiovascular disaster and are proud of it. Their food purchases are characterised by a total obliviousness to health, and a seeming lack of awareness that rationing has finished. A typical CC trolley contains salted butter, full-cream milk, sausages, huge packs of 36 economy beefburgers, oven chips, white sliced bread, microwavable cakes, Coca-Cola, and nothing organic whatsoever except possibly some apples (because the last lot have gone brown in the bowl – *See* APPLE). Right-thinking liberals refrain from damning the CC completely on the grounds that they might be genuinely unable to afford better food. This is before you watch them go to the liquor counter and buy a gross of Rothmans.

2. *Sad Bastard* SB is a single man who is utterly incapable of doing anything. His basket contains microwave food, tins, and beer. He will also buy *Family Circle* if there is an article about swimwear.

Anwar Sadat

3. *Mrs Suburbia* Mrs S likes shopping without hubby because she knows where everything is

and it's much quicker, dear. Her purchases are predominantly cleansers, bleach, washing powder and scourers etc. and she is the only person in history who has ever actually bought *Family Circle* at the checkout. Apart, of course, from Sad Bastard, but then, Mrs S doesn't buy it to masturbate over. Well, she might; we just don't know.

4. *The Guardian Weekenders* Who are these two, with the fat-free milk, the organic garlic, the multipack of Aqua Libra and the Quorn sausages? Why, it's the Guardian Weekenders, who go together to the supermarket every Saturday. He pushes the trolley while she loads it up with non-South African fruit, in the absence of a signed affidavit from the ANC saying that it's OK to buy South African fruit. They are the only people who ever buy the exotic unknown foreign vegetables; they have worked out how to eat a carambola, and buy okra, breadfruit and yams, because it helps put money back into Third World economies. In short, they are a pain in the arse.

5. *Mr Chips* This person is the opposite of the above; he will not buy anything foreign at all. The enormous expansion in the availability of exotic foods in the last fifteen years has passed him by, and he will not go within three yards of a tub of taramasalata in case he catches something. He makes an exception of the USA, because they are responsible for McCain Oven Chips. An avowed fan of Nicholas Ridley.

6. *List Fiend* The person who actually follows their shopping list. From the moment they enter the store they are buried in their piece of paper, never deviating from its instructions. No impulse, no sudden creative additions to the recipe; their life is entirely controlled and organised. Probably a divorcee or clinically insane. Or works for the Inland Revenue.

7. *Five Items Or Less* This person is utterly mad. There can be no other explanation for their behaviour. They go to a huge supermarket and queue up at the checkout with a pint of milk and a small loaf. That's it. Mad.

SUPERMARKETS; Sainsbury's pay great attention to the design of their stores

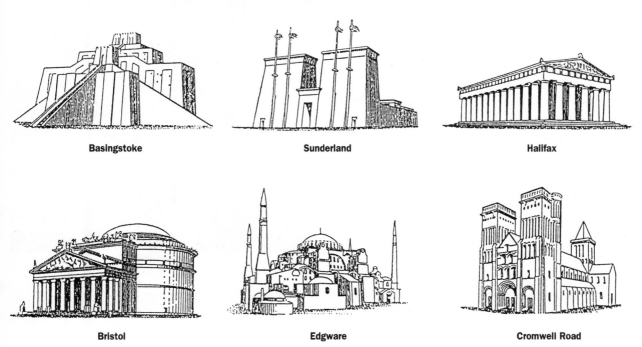

Basingstoke

Sunderland

Halifax

Bristol

Edgware

Cromwell Road

Supermarkets were the result of the retailing revolution of the 1960s, since which time there have been regular laments for the demise of the corner shop with its sense of community, its personal service and its lack of anything that you wanted to buy (unless you wanted pineapple chunks and Camp coffee.) The word super*market* is, of course, a misnomer; in none of these stores do the assistants sell fruit and veg from stalls or try and tempt you into buying stolen perfume or counterfeit Lacoste T-Shirts. Supermarkets may best be classified according to their carrier bags:

MARKS AND SPENCER FOOD STORES

The poshest of the posh. All the food is dead poncey. You don't have to do anything to any of it except stick it in the microwave (make sure you have been to a *food* store or you might have Baked Pants). The carrier bag is good to be seen with. If possible, keep it and use it for other things.

WAITROSE

Not many of them therefore quite posh. Bob Geldof shops at the one in the Kings Road. Big selection of olives and that kind of stuff. However, some of the food needs preparing a bit. Carrier bag acceptable.

SAINSBURY'S

Functional. Lots of scrubbing and peeling required. Carrier bag is sort of browny-orange colour. Throw it away as soon as you have used it.

PRESTO

Bought up by Safeway's, so the carrier bag may become a collector's item. Slogan: 'You'll be impressed in Presto.'

HAPPY SHOPPER

Enough said.

Swimming

THE BREAST STROKE

1. Posey push-off

2. Hope everyone's watching

3. Swallow mouthful of chlorine

4. Feel knackered already

Taylor, Graham I mean, for fuck's sake, is it too much to expect an England manager to get the *kit* right? Is my demand unreasonable here? The England strip is either a white shirt – and this carries a powerful psyching-out semiotic voodoo which you can translate something along the lines of : 'Yes, that's right opposition, we invented the game, and so got first pick of all the colours in the world: physics' first colour, the beginning of colour itself, the fundamental, original and principal colour. This is it: the same essential strip you saw the 1870 England team wearing in your Latin-American encyclopedia, their white 1870 shirts run effortlessly off the industrial revolution's newly mechanised looms.' Wear the white shirt and Burachaga has to deal with all that.

The England strip is either the white shirt or the *red*. The red shirt too carries its own powerful, psyching-out semiotic voodoo, which you can translate something along the lines of: 'yes, that's right: *second* pick of all colours in the world. Primary, vivid and rare: this is the red we won the World Cup in, the amazing technicolour dreamcoat with magic properties of nutter self-belief.'

Capitalising on all this, what does Graham Taylor do? Sends us out in SKY BLUE. *SKY BLUE*!!! Oh man. Of *all* colours. But then it occurred to me: *he thinks he's managing Coventry City* – and this, I think, explains some of his selection decisions. Taylor says to himself 'Ooh, I'd love to be able to pick Waddle, but then again, I suppose he's got England commitments.' (R)

Terrace, Etiquette When the crowd around you are singing 'There's Only One Neville Southall/One Neville Southall', remember not to think 'Oh, I know this one' and start singing 'Guantanamara! Quaguida Guantanmara!!' (D/R)

Thunderbirds 1960s Supermarionation series continually discussed by twenty-five to thirty-five year olds. There are many unanswered questions about International Rescue:

1. *Where was Tracey Island?* Satellite surveillance has failed to locate Tracey Island. Many people have assumed that it was situated in tropical latitudes, basing this theory on the line of collapsing palm trees on either side of *Thunderbird 2*'s runway. However, since these trees were evidently on some sort of hydraulic hinge device, capable of being raised and lowered several times a day, it is more likely that they were plastic. Supporters of the tropical-zone theory have also pointed out that the swimming pool disguising *Thunderbird 1*'s launch-bay was open-air – open-air pools being uncommon in temperate zones. However, this does not really stand up. For a start, no one was ever seen actually using the pool, for the obvious reason that there was a rocket continually coming up through it. These arguments seem to suggest that the school of thought placing Tracey Island in the Caribbean or Pacific is wrong, and that, in fact, International Rescue's headquarters was more like to be near the Scilly Isles or possi-

bly Scotland. It would need to be somewhere where private islands are readily available to buy; and given the preponderance of International Rescue cases which took place in Britain, Scotland would seem the most likely candidate. One intriguing piece of evidence is the sighting, unreported in the press, made by a Polaris submarine on a regular training mission in 1968. After strange sonar signals were received, the crew reported seeing a 'bright yellow underwater bulldozer with a 4 on the side.'

2. *How did Jeff Tracey make enough money to set up International Rescue?* The funding of the organisation has always been shrouded in mystery. Jeff Tracey was unsuccessfully investigated for tax evasion (*See* DODD SQUAD, THE) and there is some suspicion that he may have invested profits from several fraudulent City ventures in IR. Not only must International Rescue have cost a huge amount to set up, but some aspects of the operation were deliberately designed to be as costly as possible. Experts estimate development costs for *Thunderbird 2* alone at £500 million, but on top of that, we must consider that the method devised for getting Vergil into the cockpit was the most complicated method possible. Rather than have him walk up some steps into the cockpit, he has to lean against a false panel in the wall, get flipped over backwards and proceed down a long chain of chutes and conveyor belts before being deposited in his seat – a procedure privately described by Captain Scarlet as 'fucking stupid'. There is also the enormous cost of maintaining *Thunderbird 5* in space, not to mention the cost of supplying the permanently orbiting Alan Tracey with food, oxygen, pornographic magazines and Kleenex.

3. *Who was 'Brains'?* The identity of Brains is a closely-guarded secret. Clearly the technical wizard, employed to put Tracey's spare billions of pounds to good use, Brains is unlikely to be his real name. Research has proved that no one has ever graduated from any major world university in rocket engineering under the name 'Brains'. It is therefore assumed that Brains had undergone an identity-change; he may have been a Soviet defector, possibly Yuri Tropimov, the brilliant Moscow scientist who defected in 1961. The KGB were known to have him on their death-list, and this may account for his stammering nervousness when he was asked to appear on camera.

4. *Was Vergil gay?* Yes. He used to have homosexual trysts in *Thunderbird 2*. Why else was it fitted with an Automatic Camera Detector? The *News of the World* recently ran the story as

CHANNEL FIVE PUPPET PILOT POOF SHOCK

For a more detailed investigation of the *Thunderbirds* phenomenon, see J.R.Hartley's fascinating *Philanthropy meets Technology: The Story of International Rescue*. A more cynical view can be found in Kitty Kelley's acerbic *What a Bunch of Assholes – the Unauthorised Biography of the Tracey Family,* while for a simple chronological appraisal see *No Job Too Small – The Collected Missions of International Rescue 1966–70*. Individual biographies have been published of some of the team, including *E.T.A. Fifteen Minutes – The Story of Scott Tracey, I Hardly Ever Get to Do Anything – My Life as Thunderbird 3 Pilot* by Alan Tracey and *I Share My Name with A Great Roman Poet* by The Hood.

Tour de France The French are the only nation

in the world who can get worked up about cycling. It's never caught on here, although they've tried it with the Milk Race. But the average British Lad isn't convinced. Bicycles, milk – it all spells 'poof'. Now, if they could get Special Brew Lager to sponsor it instead and allow you to do wheelies and push sticks through each other's spokes, then we'd be getting somewhere. Also, there's something a bit odd about grown men wilfully riding bicycles over those sort of distances. One suspects that the Milk Race consists of hundreds of people who've all failed their driving test nine times,

and rather than admit it, they pretend that they prefer travelling round on a flimsy iron frame completely unprotected from the weather and other traffic.

The other thing about the Tour de France and the Milk Race is that the conditions under which they take place are totally artificial since *they clear the road.* Any idiot could ride a bike fast if they cleared the road. If they tried holding a section of the Milk Race through Birmingham in the morning rush-hour, then you'd see just what bicycles are really like. Three hundred bikes heading into the Inner Ring

The 1942 Tour de France. A Resistance worker surrenders to the Gestapo, robbing him of the maillot jaune

Road at 40 mph at 8.30a.m., and you'd have 300 crushed cyclists before you could say 'Raleigh Olympus'.

Tourism, British The British Tourist Board have the hardest job in the world. Since people stopped going to the seaside, they have had to try and make the rest of Britain interesting. In this quest they have opted for one simple technique – think of a new name to describe the area as this will automatically make the place more attractive. The process for choosing the name is simple: take the name of the most famous person or thing ever associated with the area and put the word country after it. For some areas this process works really well: the Yorkshire Dales use James Herriot, '*Brontë Country*' sounds a lot better than '*That bit of Yorkshire just North of Junction 12 on the M62*', and '*Catherine Cookson Country*' is a more attractive holiday destination than '*Sunderland*', which is what it actually means. Other areas, however, are nothing short

of desperate. For example, the area of East Anglia south of the Wash is now '*Hereward the Wake Country*' which is a crap slogan in anyone's book. Quite frankly, the name of an obscure Saxon king is unlikely to cause fifteen-mile tailbacks on August Bank Holiday as thousands of motorists battle with each other to reach King's Lynn and Lowestoft. Presumably this is indicative of the fact that no one famous has lived in East Anglia, although '*John Bacon, You Know, the Man Who Presents Anglia News Country*' is a possibility. However, the most desperate of all is surely Coventry, which in a last ditch attempt to escape its former image as a dull, industrial town in the West Midlands describes itself as '*The City In Shakespeare Country*', even though it's thirty miles from Stratford. Just rubbish.

Tower, Eiffel For some time the French were unsure whether to build the Eiffel Tower or not. (R)

Trainspotters

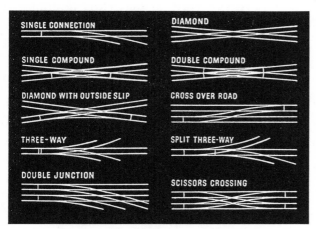

TRACK LAYOUTS; Trainspotters find these interesting

Tree Don't be fucking stupid you know what a tree is. It's a tree. You know, tree, TREE! TREE! Are you mental? It's a fucking tree. Jesus . . . (R)

Trousers

TROUSERS; Never try to get away with not wearing them

Tunnel, Channel The real question about the Channel Tunnel is: can you turn off it into

Stingray Command Base? And is Troy Tempest really the man to turn to if there is a disaster, especially considering that the concrete walls of the Tunnel are six metres thick and Stingray was four inches long and made out of plastic (and never actually went any further than the bottom of Gerry Anderson's bathtub)?[1] (R/D)

---

[1] Interestingly, in the credits to *Stingray*, Troy Tempest was seen with the beautiful mermaid Marina on a balcony under the moonlight and then later in a quiet restaurant having a romantic meal. But what it didn't show was Marina getting upset and storming out because Troy ordered fish.

Vibrator We couldn't find anything under this in *Encyclopedia Britannica* – ditto 'King-Dong Dildo' – so we got our man to come round and do the research for us:

> **VIBRATOR Phallus-like device for the artificial stimulation of sexual pleasure. The first vibrator was designed by Dr Heinrich Chartham in 1897, through the insertion of a small spontaneous combustion engine into a gramophonic cylinder, but the product did not really come into its own until the 1930s when they were first supplied with small battery-driven motors. According to the data available, these would create a buzzing-noise similar in decibels to a** . . . . *a buzzing noise . . . ?*
>
> *Sorry, where was I? I do apologise.* **Statistical data reveals that women prone to use vibrators are a) those whose husbands are likely to be involved in long periods of sedentary, cerebral, academic compilation downstairs, and b) likely eventually to take a lover from the lower classes, such as a workman.**
>
> *Excuse me a moment.*

Video Usually the whole point of having a video recorder is to record programmes which you are too busy to watch when they are actually shown. Fair enough. But if you were too busy to watch it in the first place why should you be any less busy when you want to watch the recordings? The result of this is that everyone with a video ends up with an immense stock of programmes that they will never see. This process is best illustrated when you watch the first show in a series. By the time the second show is on, you still haven't watched the first one, which means that even if you are at home you can't watch the second because that would mean watching the second before the first, which is confusing, so you have to video it instead. This means that by the third show you still haven't watched the first two and by the end of the series you have recorded all the shows, but you will never watch them because it's too much to take at one sitting and there is something else you want to watch then anyway. Even if you do make finally the monumental effort to sit down and watch it chances are that you haven't recorded it properly anyway and instead of the all important first ten minutes of the programme you wanted what you have actually got is the last ten minutes of an extended *Nine O'clock News,* an item on an organic chicken farm in Norwich, and Suzanne Charlton standing in front of a satellite picture of some clouds.

		FABRIC CARE GUIDE
	Programme	**Examples of Application**
95	**Bloody Hot**	White cotton and linen - no special finish. White sheets with dubious stains. Horrid jumpers you were given for Christmas and want to shrink so you don't have to wear them anymore. ***Will make your pants go blue***
60	**Very Hot**	Coloured sheets with dubious stains. Duvet covers with dubious stains. Sports kit you found at the bottom of that carrier bag with the mould all over it. Woollens if you still don't know how to use the washing machine. Particularly horrid socks. ***Will make your pants go blue***
40	**Luke Warm**	Absolutely everything else. If you are too crap to read all those little labels just bung it in at about this temperature. ***Will still make your pants go blue***
10	**Pointlessly Cold**	If you want things to be dirty even though you've washed them. If your washing is being filmed for a soap powder comparison test.
	Handwash	When something is so dirty you want to wash it in the privacy of your own bathroom. When the washing machine is knackered, you've run out of pants and you don't have the right coins for the launderette.

Mixed Load Washing Instructions: Select lowest temperature on all the labels, use medium wash cycle for your selected temperature. (See manufacturers instructions.) Your pants will still go blue.

Fabric Care General Advice

Do Not Tumble Dry

Do Not Bleach

Do Not Leave Tissue in Pocket

It might be a good idea to iron this if you could be bothered

Your washing machine is broken

This washing is too dirty. Throw it away.

Waddle, What About a Water-bottle

Waddle, What About a Water-bottle Punchline of joke I really liked when I was four. Lord Ponsonby-Smythe is in the bath, and, to cut a long story short, he farts. Next thing you know, in comes his butler, Waddle, with a water-bottle. Lord Ponsonby-Smythe says 'What did you bring that in for?' and Waddle says 'Well, sir, I

distinctly heard you say "What about a water-bottle, Waddle?"'

There is another version of the joke I made up. Lord Ponsonby-Smythe is in the bath and farts as before, only this time his butler is called Water-bottle. Two seconds later, in comes Water-bottle walking like a duck. 'Why are you walking like a duck?' says Lord Ponsonby-Smythe. 'Well, sir' says Water-bottle, 'I distinctly heard you say "What about a waddle, Water-bottle?" '

Are we really getting paid £50,000 for this? (D)

Washing Machines The most difficult thing is working out how on earth to use them (see opposite).

Weddings All weddings are pretty much the same, really. When you get to the church you'll be given an Order of Service, and it'll probably read like the one on the next page.

Wedgie Often carried out by groups of drunken

WEDGIE; London, 1938: Jack "The Razor" Gibson in potential pre-wedgie situation.
Vicious gang-war wedgings were often carried out in British Home Stores changing cubicles

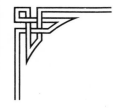

BARRY AND CHRISTINE
13.6.91

THE WEDDING SERVICE

Music:
Albinoni Canon in D

(The Congregation Shall Look Around and Say 'The Last Time I Was in a Church Must've Been Oh, What, About Three Years Ago for That Carol Service.')

The Entrance of the Bride
Music:
Here Comes the Bride (trad)

(The Congregation Shall Stand and Whisper 'Oooh, doesn't she look lovely' Except for Auntie June Who Shall Whisper 'Of course, she's rather plain under all that make-up.)

Hymn 49 To Be A Pilgrim (Christine Used to Like it at School)

He who would valiant be 'gainst all disaster
Let him in constancy follow the Master
There's no discouragement shall make him once relent
His First avowed intent, to be a pilgrim

Whoso would set him round, . . . er da da dum dum dum
Laa la la . . . er . . . um . . . . follow the Master
There's no . . . discour . . . er what . . . no, I don't know them either
His first . . . It was a long time ago . . . to be a pilgrim.

(Verses 3–6 will be sung by the Vicar alone, whilst everyone hums, or looks embarrassed.)

The Marriage
(The Congregation Shall Kneel. Although, In Fact, Most of Them Will Just Lean Forward in Their Pews and Hope No One Notices.)

The Minister shall ask if anyone knows any cause or just impediment why Barry and Christine should not be joined in holy matrimony.
(The Congregation Shall Keep a Straight Face Even Though They Know They Have Both Put It About a Bit.)

The Giving of the Ring
(The Best Man Shall Step Forward Trying to Disguise His Monstrous Hangover and Present The Ring – £19.99 at Ratners.)

The Vows and Zooming-in of the Video Camera

The Entrance of Gary And Kevin from The Pub
(The Congregation Shall Try and Ignore the Argument at the Back of the Church As Gary and Kevin Finally Make It From The King's Arms.)

The Address
The Vicar advises Barry and Christine on how difficult living together will be sometimes, revealing to the congregation that he doesn't know they have already lived together for three years.

Hymn All things Bright and Beautiful
(All thirteen Verses Sung Much Too Slowly To the Other Tune That Nobody Knows.)

All things bright and beautiful
All creatures great and small
All things wise and wonderful
The Lord God made them all (Refrain)

Da da da da dum look how many verses there are
I'm getting a bit peckish now (etc.)

The Signing of the Register
Music
A Medley of Christine's Favourite Hits
Lady In Red (De Burgh)
The Power of Love (J. Rush)
The Music From That Pirelli Advert (Puccini)

(The Bride and Groom Shall Disappear into the Vestry and the Congregation Shall Chat Loudly About How Much It Costs to Have a Wedding Nowadays.)

The Prayers
(The Congregation Shall Shuffle Uncomfortably in Their Seats.)

The Procession
Music
The Wedding March (Mendelssohn)
Killed by Death (Motorhead)

(Christine's Mum Shall Blow Her Nose. All Young Women in the Congregation Shall Get Nudged by Older Relatives Who Shall Say 'Your Turn Soon'.)

The Photographs
No one shall be let out of the church until Barry and Christine have had 500 photos taken at the Church door.
(All shall Then Proceed to Local Function Suite for Bad Speeches and Bitchy remarks about the Cheapness of the Catering.There Shall be Risque Jokes about Wedding Nights despite the fact that the Bride and Groom having Been having Sex for Six Years.)

The Tying of the Cans to Barry's XR3i.

rugby players, the *wedgie* is the lifting up of an innocent victim by the underpants until the elastic breaks. The broken pants are then hung ceremoniously from the nearest lampshade, while the victim writhes on the floor in agony. The possibility of being *wedgied,* however remote, is one of the strongest arguments for not wearing the structurally stronger swimming trunks when you have run out of clean pants.

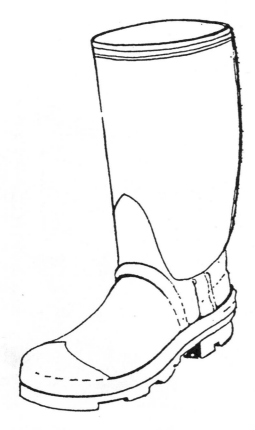

WELLINGTON BOOT; Named after a Duke, worn by wankers with Range Rovers

Wellington Boot It does the Duke of Wellington no credit that he invented these. He ought to be remembered for saving Europe from the threat of Napoleonic conquest, and masterminding one of the great military victories of all time, a victory which shaped the map of Europe for the nineteenth century. Quite frankly, thinking of him spending his spare time standing in ponds with a jam jar rather takes the edge off.

W. G. Grace If he was such a good cricketer, how come he only had a toy bat? (R)

W.G. Grace

Whale Nation Classic conservation poem by Heathcote Williams. I have made some corrections. (R)

Out of the body of one whale
Is made oil, jewellery, clothes, medicine, soap, furniture, cosmetics and ornaments . . .
What a bargain:
Try getting all that lot out of a panda.

Oh whale,
Research shows you have a language
Twice as sophisticated as modern English;
And yet you spend the whole time saying
'Wheee! Coooo! Wheeee!'

'I told you it was him who stole the sausages.' A kleptomaniac whale is apprehended in the high street.

Oh whale,
You are equipped with a natural sonar radar,
Far more advanced than modern technology.
I, on the other hand, equipped with a Nicholson
Streetfinder and a poor sense of direction,
Have yet to park my car underneath a polar ice cap.

You think you're so clever with your one party trick:
Farting out the top of your head,
In two years' time there will be no more pandas,
And then you're next.

Wheelbarrow Useful in the garden.

**Once you have mastered the technique,
pushing a wheelbarrow can provide hours of fun**

Window If you don't know what one of these is, then it looks like it'll have to be another ten years in your special school, putting your hands first in hot then cold water with a member of staff there to monitor for any flicker of reaction, and safely surrounded by brightly coloured bouncy objects. (R)

Windscreen Boy, there's such a lot of things you have to put in an encyclopedia. Whew . . . windscreen linscreen, dinsqueemm . . . .

Wogan, Terry Terry Wogan was born on the 3 June 1854. His first words were: 'It's not a wig.' Soon he grew a full head of hair, but carried on wearing a wig. He first became a TV personality on *Blankety Blank*, but left the programme after

one of the cards came up with the puzzle 'Sir Terence of Wogan once lost all his hair and had to wear a blank.'

Tragically, Terry's pretence of hair-ownership has always been flawed by the fact that his name sounds a little bit like 'Wig-On'. In fact, this *is* his real name, and his middle name is 'I've Got A' – Terry I've Got A Wig-On. This, of course, is a bit of a giveaway, although it helped him in his early career, when he was invited to present a similar show to *Vision On*, the programme for the deaf, called *Wig On*, for the blind. Similarly, you may have heard of the Tom Hanks film *Big*. Terry was once in a similar film called *Wig*. In *Big*, Tom Hanks, an adult man, magically becomes a child; in *Wig*, Terry Wogan, a bald man, magically grows a full head of hair.

But keeping up the façade has not always been easy, and there have been times when Terry has felt a desperate desire to confess. For example, it was only after much persuasion that he agreed to change the title of his one chart hit, 'The Floral Dance', from its original title, 'All Right, I'm Bald.' Terry is also thought to be a member of a secret society of top celebrities who all wear wigs, and who meet at a secret address in London, where the hairpieces are collected at the door, and the celebrities may circulate unencumbered and scalp-naked: this place is known as 'The Wigless Club'.

Mr Wogan has been criticised for touching women on the bare knee, but what must be remembered is that he probably thinks he's scratching his head. Perhaps the final recognition came with the granting of an entry in *Who's Who*:

WOGAN, TERRY: TV chat-show host. 2d. Interests: Going to the barbers, twice, maybe four times a week, buying shampoo, cartwheeling, going swimming without worrying about it, using a blow-dryer without checking that the windows are closed first, and taking his hat off without then looking in the inside of the hat.

(R/D)

Work The idea that you are supposed to work for a living is the big lie of human history. It's extraordinary that before venturing on a career, more people don't think 'What? I'm supposed to go to the same place every day and have a really unpleasant time – and I'm supposed to do this non-stop until six months before I die? Fuck off!'

There is no better example of the damage total dedication to work can do than Japan. The Japanese economic miracle seems to have been achieved, as far as can be ascertained from the game show *Endurance*, at the cost of all human decency. Although considering Japanese people are so keen on sado-masochism, *Endurance* would probably be more worthy of the name if it involved them having to be nice to each other for more than five seconds.[1]

Part of this confusion over work in this country has been caused by the TV programme *Troubleshooter* – the show where Sir John Harvey-Jones turns up at a different company each week and tells them what they're doing wrong and how it should be run. (Incredibly, so far no company boss has gone ''Ave you finished mate?' and kicked his head in.) What Sir John should be doing of course is telling you how to *avoid* working. Here's a few suggested ideas for the next series:

(D/R)

```
Program 1: How to be the One in a Group
of Five People Carrying A Heavy Weight
Who Isn't Actually Carrying It.

ENTER SIR JOHN

Sir John: This you achieve by grunting
and frowning and maybe even stopping
and flapping your arms in the air.
Goodnight.

EXIT SIR JOHN


Program 2: How To Avoid Doing Something
That Someone Tells You To Do.

ENTER SIR JOHN

Sir John: Stand around for a while
looking like you'd rather not and
eventually he'll say 'Oh all right then
don't bother.'
```

[1] You do sometimes see a version of this on the TV. For some reason, it's normally two very fat blokes, and they get about as far as bowing to each other, which I suppose is quite nice, but then straight away they start fighting

Fly Wright Brothers
The World's No.1 Airline

FLY TO DESTINATIONS ABOUT 75 YARDS UP THE FIELD.

EACH OF OUR PLANES IS EQUIPPED WITH LAWN MOWER ENGINES AND FLIES AT AN ALTITUDE OF TEN FEET. THE WINGS COLLAPSE ON LANDING.

THROUGHOUT THE FLIGHT YOU WILL BE ACCOMPANIED BY SOME NEW YORK TIMES JOURNALISTS ON BICYCLES.

OTHER DESTINATIONS WHICH WRIGHT BROTHERS WILL BE

OFFERING INTO 1902 – OFF A PIER AND INTO THE SEA.

JUST HOPPING OFF THE GROUND FOR A FEW SECONDS. SOMETIMES FOR AS LONG AS SEVEN SECONDS, THOUGH.

W B A

Wright Brothers Invented and flew first aeroplane. Also first pioneers of airflight to exploit commercial side of flying, realising its potential as the luxury transport of the twentieth century.

Wrong Number Callers Phone callers who don't know me by name always say 'Rapid Express?' Ten or twenty phone calls ago, a woman asked me how long it would take to get a parcel by motorbike to Halifax in West Yorkshire. I thought for a bit and said: 'You've asked me one there. What is it, about 300 miles to Yorkshire? So it'd probably be about four hours, I suppose, depending on the traffic. Although, come to think of it, the advantage of a motorbike, over say a van or a car, is that they can nip in and out of traffic jams on busy motorways. If it was a very large parcel, though, it might make the bike wobble around a lot and have to go pretty slowly. It would also depend what cc bike it was. I mean I've seen some around that are as much as 1300cc – I bet they could shift a bit, eh? Now why don't you just fuck off?' (R)

Wrong Number Dialling That You Do Yourself Not one of my cunting friends lives within a fifty-mile radius of me. Stevie Welford – ma bezzie – lives in Turin. Whenever I dial him, tho', some fault on the line or Mediterranean fault-line connects me faithfully to la famiglia Andreoli. (My bill breakdown's God's headache: 'I can't figure it out – he's making regular calls to a family I haven't got him down with at all. Send Calvin up here, I want a word.') Every single time I try and phone, I get connected up with the Andreolis. They've got no English, me no Italian. I wish I did know some. Then perhaps I could help, because they seem to be going through some crisis, they sound terrible. Something's upsetting them. In fact, each time I've called up this week, say since call 28 or 29 on, it seems to have got worse. It's certainly a time of rising tension in the Andreoli household.

Tragically, they're pouring their problems out to someone powerless to understand, and yet, as far as I can make out, I'm the only person they can really open up to about it. They seem to keep it all bottled up until I call (very un-Italian). But then I say 'Hello, it's me, just seeing how you were' – and it's the full waterworks.

I just wish I could share it with them. What I lack in language though, I make up in devotion. I'll call back a couple of times more later tonight just to let them know that someone out there cares. To see if they sound any calmer, or have at least stopped screaming. It's 2a.m. now. However, I seem to remember two facts about Italy:
1) they're an hour ahead of us
and
2) they think we're cunts. (R)

Xenophobia See entry under 'Yurt' below.

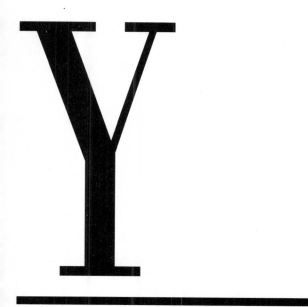

Yak Big animal. Migrates in large herds and is intensely interested in the modern novel.

THE YAK; Notoriously difficult to draw

Yes Archetypal pomp-rock band. They wrote songs with titles like 'Heart of the Sunrise' 'Siberian Khatru' and 'Tales from Topographic Oceans'. They got their name from the answer they constantly found themselves giving to journalists who asked 'Aren't these titles just a tad pretentious?'

Y-Fronts Undergarments worn by men. Available either in plain white, coloured or with a crap logo on the front.

LONG VEHICLE

BEWARE OF THE BEAST

I HAVE A VERY LARGE PENIS

Yikes Phrase used only by characters in cartoons. Similarly, phrases like 'Grrrr', 'Wh-o-o-o-o-ah!' and 'Wha...whassat?'

Yurt A type of tent-dwelling found in Mongolia. Ulan Bator's full of them. They're not all that great, to be honest, but if you want to live in Ulan Bator, you're not going to get a four-storey Georgian townhouse with all original features and custom-built Smallbone kitchen, are you? No – you're going to get a yurt. You could always install a custom-built kitchen, but to be honest, the average Mongolian isn't really going to know the difference between Smallbone and Hygena, or one of the cheaper Schreibers. So you could save yourself a few bob there, and buy an extra goat.

Zebedee In *The Magic Roundabout* Zebedee was the one with the big black moustache and a spring instead of legs. At the end of the programme he would appear with a 'dyyyyong' noise and say 'Time for Bed'. Whether or not this had a sexual connotation is not certain. Zebedee could well have been addressing this to Florence, but it's hard to see how he could hope for any sort of realistic sexual relationship when he had a spring instead of legs. Possibly theirs was a non-penetrative relationship. Or maybe Zebedee was a New Man and had decided to have a contraceptive coil fitted to him rather than Florence.

Zebra Looks like a horse, but it has black-and-white stripes, which help it camouflage itself in the green-and-brown veldts of central Africa. Living proof that evolution sometimes totally cocks it up.

Zenda No idea where this is, but there's a prison there, presumably.

Zoo Zoos were invented in the days before David Attenborough, and this accounts for both their political and emotional unacceptability,

A cunningly-disguised Shergar enjoying his new life in Kenya

and the fact that they're generally tawdry and horrible. The fact is that, if you want to see hippos copulating or three-toed sloths demonstrating how they lick between their toes, you can buy a video of *Life on Earth*. What there is no point in doing is going and peering through some rusty wire fence at a hut and a pile of straw while your parents say, 'It's inside at the moment. It'll come out in a minute.'

The impact of TV on zoos has meant that most zoos have had to turn themselves into a theme park with some animals in. Chessington Zoo is now called Chessington World of Adventures largely because kids in the 1990s are more interested in travelling on a monorail than watching a giraffe having a shit. Which it invariably did. In fact, all the animals did. All you ever saw, as you went round the zoo, was dilating anuses and globs of smelly brown matter hitting the concrete. This also meant that zoos smelt of poo. And this is another reason why it's better to see animals on telly — because you don't have to smell their poo.

Of course, one interesting thing that could happen at the zoo would be that you might see a male animal with an erection, and this was good for embarrassing your parents with. It was always a good laugh to have to watch the elephant wandering around with an enormous stiffy, while mum and dad hurriedly decided it was time for an ice cream.

Appendix I

Dear Mary Whitehouse Experience,

As someone who enjoys nothing more than a good bar of chocolate, I would like in the most strongest terms to point out that since I read this joke, I can no longer eat *Turkish Delight* without feeling that I am in some sense stimulating a Turkish tradesman's enormous organ.

Yours gratefully

Marc Almond.

P.S. I've recently put on fifteen stone.

Appendix 2

Dear Mary Whitehouse Experience,

I am a glamour model getting regular work in *Sneaky Peeks*, *Shaven Ravers* and the whole *Parade* range (touch wood). I deeply object to the suggestion that I might not work under my real name.

Yours,

Desiree Titfeel

P.S. Could you put me in touch with a recommended swimming pool cleaner?

SPORTING RECORDS

ASSOCIATION FOOTBALL

Football League Champions

1971-72	Stoke City	1981-82	Stoke City
1972-73	Stoke City	1982-83	Stoke City
1973-74	Stoke City	1983-84	Stoke City
1974-75	Stoke City	1984-85	The Shit
1975-76	Stoke City	1985-86	Stoke City
1976-77	Stoke City	1986-87	Stoke City
1977-78	Stoke City	1987-88	Stoke City
1978-79	Stoke City	1988-89	Stoke City
1979-80	Stoke City	1989-90	Stoke City
1980-81	Stoke City	1990-91	Stoke City

F.A.Cup Winners

1971-72	Stoke City	1981-82	Stoke City
1972-73	Stoke City	1982-83	Stoke City
1973-74	Stoke City	1983-84	Stoke City
1974-75	Stoke City	1984-85	Stoke City
1975-76	Stoke City	1985-86	Stoke City
1976-77	Stoke City	1986-87	Stoke City
1977-78	Stoke City	1987-88	Stoke City
1978-79	Stoke City	1988-89	Stoke City
1979-80	Stoke City	1989-90	Stoke City
1980-81	Stoke City	1990-91	Port Vale

World Cup Winners

1950	Uruguay	1974	Stoke City
1954	Stoke City	1978	Stoke City
1958	Stoke City	1982	Stoke City
1962	Stoke City	1986	Stoke City
1966	Stoke City	1990	Stoke City
1970	Stoke City		

INDEX OF THINGS NOT INCLUDED IN THIS ENCYCLOPEDIA

Aachen (*But see* DULL GERMAN TOWNS

Abacus

Abutement

Accrington Stanley

Adding machine (*See* CRAP THINGS)

Aeoli

Ajax (*See* TROJAN WAR, SANITARY ARRANGMENTS OF)

Alicante

Amias, Jeremy

Amis, Martin

Abracadabra

Abysmally Poor Sitcoms

Bathmat

Bloo-Loo

Barry, John (*See* JOHN, BARRY)

Bostik

Boston

Bad Manners (*See* FATTY, LIPPING-UP OF)

Bugle

Beezer

Beazer Homes League

Boogie Wonderland

Burt Bacharach

Belle and Sebastian

Big Jim Jehosophat

Beat, Hey – What's This? It's Got A Good

Biryani, King Prawn

Cotton, Dot

Cod (*See* FISH THAT HAVE HAD WARS NAMED AFTER THEM)

Carp (*See* THE CARP WAR OF 1873)

Chin-Rub

Coypu

Chung, Wang (*See* WANG, CHUNG)

Charlton, Suzanne (*See* MEMBERS OF 1966 WORLD CUP-WINNING ENGLAND TEAM WITH METEOROLOGIST OFFSPRING)

Crew, Kath

Curd, Graham

Cybermen

Cholet, Madam

Def Leppard (*See* FAMOUS AMPUTEE DRUMMERS)

Def (*See* BEETHOVEN)

Dolenz, Mickey

Droitwich

Derek Smalls

Dill the Dog

Eggs

E.S.P

Emulsion Paint (*See* PAINT, NON-GLOSS)

Emu (*See* REALLY VERY FUNNY HANDPUPPETS)

Ecu (*See* REALLY VERY FUNNY CURRENCIES)

Exfoliation

Excruciating (*See* SITCOM)

EMF

EtonHogg, Sir Denis

Father Dear Father

Funny Faces

Frampton Comes Alive!

Fetlocks (*See* WORDS THAT SOUND A BIT LIKE 'BOLLOCKS')

Funkytown, Won't You Take Me To

Fogg, Willy

Fatbelly Jones

Follyfoot

Friday, Freaky

Gannet

Gormenghast

Gas Bills

Gudgeon

Get Carter

Generate, Let's Meet the 8 Who Are Going To

Ha-Ha, Harvey

Haddock (*See* THE HADDOCK WAR OF 1788)

Hurst, Geoff (*See* MEMBERS OF 1966 WORLD CUP-WINNING ENGLAND TEAM WITHOUT METEOROLOGIST OFFSPRING)

Haydock (*See* RACECOURSES WITH NAMES THAT SOUND A BIT LIKE 'HADDOCK')

Hamlet

Harket, Morten

Hammer, MC

Hammer, Jan

Hammer, Mike

Holly, You Know the Computer off of *Red Dwarf*

Hoover, Jimmy the

Histamines

Hi Ho Silver Lining

Humphrey About (Watch Out, Watch Out, Watch Out There's A)

Ice-T

Ink

Indianapolis

Inkspots

If A Picture Paints A Thousand Words

Jethro Tull

Janitor

Jump (*See* HALEN, VAN; CAMERA, AZTEC; BEAMON, BOB)

Jazzy Jeff

Job, The Italian

Junkers

James, Sid

Just Juice

Kempton Park (*See* RACECOURSES WITH NAMES THAT DON'T SOUND LIKE FISH)

Kipper (*See* FISH WITH NAMES THAT DON'T SOUND LIKE RACECOURSES)

Kipling, Mr

Kit

Kit-Kat

Kitty, Kitty, Here

Loop-di-Love

Love Comes in Spurts

Love is Like Oxygen

Lite, Dee

Lithium

Lick My Love Pump

Lee, Leapy

Large

Little

Lopsided, Mrs

Mango

Mandingo

Mind Your Language (*See* THAT BLOKE OFF OF MIND YOUR LANGUAGE)

Manganese Sulphate

Muppet Show

Mouskouri, Nana

Mondays, Happy

Muskehounds, Dogtanian & the

McQuickly, Dirk

Ne-ne-na-na-na-na-nu-nu (*See* BAD MANNERS)

Nixon, David

Nixon, Richard

Ninety-Nine Red Balloons
Nena
Nesquik, Banana –
Nebula
Nobcheese
Noone, Peter
Nutrasweet
Nellie the Elephant
Nessun Dorma
Osterly (*See* PICCADILLY LINE
  WESTBOUND)
Osibisa
Oprah Winfrey
Oh No, It's Selwyn Froggit
  (*See* THINGS THAT SHOULDN'T BE IN
  THIS INDEX)
Okra
Omo
Ox-Bow Lake
Oxo (*See* ADVERTS, NAUSEATING)
Parkas, Merton
PM Dawn
Parker
Picasso
Pertwee, Jon
Paxman, Jeremy
Paxo
Pig
Pi
Pie
Pye
Pee
Poo
Poo Poo
Potty Time
Query
Querulous
Question Time
Queen Mother
Queeg
Rover Biscuit Assortment
Rover 800 series
Rowlf
Ramprakash
Redbridge
Red Sky At Night, Shepherd's
  Delight (*See* also RED SKY IN
  MORNING, SHEPHERD'S WARNING)
Reasons To Be Cheerful, Pt 3
Racey Rin Tin Tin
Red Sky in Morning, Shepherd's
  Warning (*See* also RED SKY AT
  NIGHT, SHEPHERD'S DELIGHT; RED

SKY IN MID-AFTERNOON, MAJOR
  VOLCANIC ACTIVITY IN UPPER
  ATMOSPHERE)
St. Hubbins, David
Samovar
Satire
Sea-Urchin
Septic Tank
Splits, Banana (*See* FLEEGO; BINGO;
  DROOPER & SNORK)
Sputum
Swordfish (*See* FISH THAT ARE NAMED
  AFTER SHARP OBJECTS)
Spikefish (*See above*)
Supersonic
Spud-u-Like
Spedding, Chris
Seal Cull
Sex Dwarf
Scoreboard, Let's Have A Look At
  The Old
Savage, Viv
Sexy Clip
Sedentary Occupation
Seaside Special
Skolar, When You Know Lager
  You're A
Sexton, Dave
Tufnell, Nigel
Tucker's Luck
Tuba, Tubby the
Typically Tropical
T-Rex
Trex
Things That Make You Go Hmmm
Trousers, Short
Twirl, Give Us A
Troughton, Patrick
Temptations, The
Totting-ham, In the Cup for (*See*
  ARDILES, OSSIE)
Tomsk
Turtle, Touché
Trout (*See* TROUT WARS 1624-7)
Trotsky
UNCLE, Man From
Ullapool
Ustinov, Percy
Usk
United Airlines
United, Ham, West
United, Sheffield
United, If the Kids Are

United, Re- (*See* PEACHES AND HERB)
Vauxhall Nova
V.D.
Vicks Sinex (*See* MALCOLM)
Vicious, Sid
Vimto
Vern, Big
Vim
Venables, Terry
Vegetables, Terry
Vodaphone
Van Morrison
Varney, Reg
Whopping the Bishop
Wasted Youth
Wonka, Willy
Well, Didn't He Do?
Wellington (*See* DEFEAT OF
  NAPOLEON; THE ROLE OF THE
  WOMBLES)
X-Ray Spex
Xenon
Yis!
Yo!
Yoghurt
Yog
Yoda, You Know the Bloke off of
  Star Wars with the Big Ears
Yodelling (*See* SILLY THINGS TO DO
  IN THE ALPS)
Yootha Joyce
Zany Ade
ZZ Top (*See* BEARDS)
Zippy-Dee Doo Dah, Zippity Ay
Zed and Two Noughts
Zounds